Testimonials

Tanja's book brilliantly addresses the psychological challenges women often encounter in male-dominated industries. Her focus on assertiveness, self-awareness, and resilience is essential for women looking to excel in consulting. This book is more than just career advice—it provides the mental tools necessary for lasting success and well-being in a demanding field.

— Dr. Bianca Serwinski,
Chartered Psychologist, Associate Professor
and Head of Psychology at University

Tanja's engaging and insightful journey through the world of Big Four consulting reveals one powerful truth: consulting is a gateway to limitless opportunities. Through her witty storytelling and practical advice, she offers invaluable lessons of growth for ambitious young women determined to make their mark in any corporate environment—whether large or small. #girlconsultant also teaches aspiring talent, regardless of gender, how to train and leverage this skill-set for (financial) success across any future professional endeavors—whether as entrepreneurs or as leading professionals transitioning across industries. This book is a must-read for anyone with big dreams seeking a head start to strategically build their career.

— Dina Holzapfel,
Serial Entrepreneur & Life-Long Learner

Given the myriad of books out there for consultants, few have been able to combine domain knowledge, common interpersonal and career challenges, questions of day to day client work and all that from the perspective of women: in a witty, light hearted manner. Working in tech consulting within the field of AI, this book is on-point in the issues it touches upon, doing so astutely, while making me laugh out loud. This is the brilliance of the book. To not be preachy, provide perspective and make for good reading while simultaneously providing actionable and practical advice. This is why the book reels you in, gives you "aha" moments and hopefully convinces you to join consulting!

— Beenish Waris,
Head of Department in Tech Consulting for Data and AI

As someone who has navigated through various manufacturing businesses, I recognize the value of strong, capable consultants in helping drive strategic initiatives. Tanja's book is not only a practical guide for those entering consulting but also a roadmap for cultivating leadership qualities through assertiveness critical to transform businesses. Her insights provide any woman aiming to influence and shape the future of organizations with a unique take on how this journey can be explored in consulting with a lot of humor and banter.

— Clarah Manuhwa, woman in engineering,
Global Director at a leading manufacturing
firm headquartered in Switzerland

Tanja's book is a powerful resource for women who want to succeed in consulting while staying true to themselves. Women often underestimate themselves at work so her focus on authenticity, confidence, and personal growth resonates deeply with the principles I teach my coachees. With tools like assertive communication, this book empowers its readers to live more fulfilling lives both professionally and personally.

— Usman Ramay,
Senior Amazon Executive & Leadership Coach

#girlconsultant

#girlconsultant

A Woman's Playbook to Jumpstart a Career in Business Consulting

By

TANJA DEISLER

PYP Publish Your Purpose

For permission requests, write to the publisher, addressed "Attention: Permissions Coordinator," at the address below.

Publish Your Purpose
141 Weston Street, #155
Hartford, CT, 06141

Publish
Your Purpose

The opinions expressed by the Author are not necessarily those held by Publish Your Purpose.

Ordering Information: Quantity sales and special discounts are available on quantity purchases by corporations, associations, and others. For details, contact the author at thegirlconsultant@gmail.com

Edited by: Connie Mayse, Emily Ribeiro
Cover design by: Nelly Murariu
Typeset and e-book design by: Amit Dey

ISBN: 979-8-88797-139-1 (hardcover)
ISBN: 979-8-88797-140-7 (paperback)
ISBN: 979-8-88797-141-4 (ebook)

Library of Congress Control Number: 2024913792

First edition, March 2025

The information contained within this book is strictly for informational purposes. The material may include information, products, or services by third parties. As such, the Author and Publisher do not assume responsibility or liability for any third-party material or opinions. The publisher is not responsible for websites (or their content) that are not owned by the publisher. Readers are advised to do their own due diligence when it comes to making decisions.

Publish Your Purpose is a hybrid publisher of non-fiction books. Our mission is to elevate the voices often excluded from traditional publishing. We intentionally seek out authors and storytellers with diverse backgrounds, life experiences, and unique perspectives to publish books that will make an impact in the world. Do you have a book idea you would like us to consider publishing? Please visit PublishYourPurpose. com for more information.

Table of Contents

Dedication

For the girl consultants who dare to dream big and push boundaries—this book is for you. May it inspire you to realize just how powerful you truly are.

Call to Action

For additional material and to join the #girlgang visit:
https://girlconsultant.com/

A letter to all the #girlconsultants,

Hey, future #girlconsultant,

How lovely to meet you. I am Tanja. I started my consulting career in my early 20s, in Germany, specializing in supply chain and engineering. Generally, there are not many women in engineering, let alone in consulting in engineering. Thus, I am not your average Josephine, and this is not your average book. I am guessing you are not average either if you are considering consulting.

Excellent. Looks like we are already two birds of a feather . . . I am your narrator, or tour guide, if you will, who will usher you through this book. I am your gal-pal, someone who has lived through a lot of situations—which I will share with you, no matter how embarrassing they are. But don't be fooled. We will talk about the lessons I have learned along the way, and we will also dive into theory, concepts, definitions, and other unsexy things that I promise you are useful and equally as important as an aspiring stellar #girlconsultant.

I was a successful girl consultant, and in the seven years that I worked for a Big 4, I earned a pretty decent salary for my early 20s. I worked in multiple countries all around Europe; I had gold status at the major airlines and hotel chains. I went on to get my current employment as a result of the years that I spent in consulting.

Not only that—while I was consulting, I started my own clothing and apparel line. The thing is that this book is not about how successful I was in consulting. This book is about showing you how I learned all these things the hard way so you don't have to. There are not a lot of stories here about me tooting my own horn, but you will also read about the stops I made on the struggle bus.

My intention with this book is to help you be successful. I want to tell you everything you need to know to excel in your first two years in consulting. However, this is not a PhD thesis, so some topics are touched upon lightly. I am here to cheer you on, build up your confidence, and remind you what an amazing and capable person you are. Now, we may not be best friends yet, but we will be by the end of this book. Speaking of the book . . . let me give you a short tour.

I have clustered this book into four parts, and depending on where you are in your consulting career (e.g., you may be looking to get into consulting; or you may have already secured a job and are now wondering what your first project may look like), I have just the right material to help you make an informed decision on what your next step could look like.

In the first part of this book, I focus on how to get into consulting, what consulting is, and the different types of consulting companies. I have written this part for anyone who is interested in giving consulting a go, but doesn't quite know how to tackle the process. Some of the things I will tell you cannot be found on any company's website; these are things you would only notice once you are working in consulting. Here are some examples of things that no one tells you: the pros and cons between the different types of consulting companies, what impact they may have on your career, and the different paths you can take within the industry. Basically, I know the tea and I am serving it HOT. (And not just in this section of the book, but through every section . . .)

The second part is about how to crack the interview. Consulting companies have their own format for interviews, which I will deconstruct, explaining each piece so you can nail your interview. I will go into the theory of the interview, and I will elaborate on my successful (and not so successful) interviews to provide a good picture of what an interview really looks like and to show that it is okay if you bomb. Since my aim is also to help you get ahead, and statistics say that women in general don't negotiate their salaries, I will tell you about the contract, what to watch out for, what the standard models are (overtime, no overtime), and what a signing bonus is.

In the third part of the book, I'll address things that will be helpful to you once you have started in consulting, setting you up for success. A large chunk of this section dives really deeply into assertiveness. Understanding assertiveness will help you maneuver nearly everything at work, no matter where you are in the world. You'll also come to understand you don't have to be outgoing to be assertive, nor super confident. Everyone can be assertive. Through being assertive and being able to spot assertiveness in other people, you will realize that most people's behaviors are a reflection of them, not you. This will then give you more peace of mind and help you deal with stress so much better. In the latter half of this section, I review hard and soft skills—the ones I think are the most important to your consulting career and those that will serve you even if you decide to change career paths.

The fourth part focuses on what it means to be a woman in consulting, because last time I checked, we did not have gender equality YET, and there are ways to maneuver the terrain that the men in consulting don't have to think about. In these chapters, I will help you navigate the world of consulting, from playing good company politics to staying authentic at the same time; from knowing what to consider when dressing for work, without falling into centuries old, old-fashioned dos and don'ts. Plus, I will share my travel tips, because after so much time on the road, I have a few. And lastly, I will share how consulting empowered me to start my own fashion label, called Corner Office, because once you've got lots of mad skills you realize how much else you might be capable of.

Before we are through, I assume you and I will be real friends. I will have told you some of my secrets, some of my most embarrassing stories, just like true-blue friends do. You will probably think: How could any of these be true? But it all happened.

Now, as you read each chapter, be on the lookout for the ending pieces. Each chapter will end with a *tl;dr* (too long/didn't read) part, where I summarize the chapters in bullet points, in true consulting manner. Of course, it will be so much more fun to read the chapter, but that's up to you! You may also come across some other fun and informative feature boxes throughout the chapters, such as:

Tea Time:

The T in "tea" stands for truth; here I will share my real-life consulting stories.

If you don't know, now you know:

These callouts are for terms or ideas that may be new for you.

#girlconsultant life hacks:

These boxes highlight one or two sentences, because we hope you'll write that stuff down or commit it to memory. They are totally shareable, so if you post them to social media, too, I'd love that—just make sure you tag me so we can give you a virtual high-five for sharing the love (and the knowledge)!

Now, you may be wondering, how did it come about that I am sharing so much of my knowledge and so many of my own stories? Well, it all began in my first year in consulting. I always loved writing and I started an anonymous blog: #thegirlconsultant. Through that blog, I shared all I had learned with a community of young women. Over the years, I accumulated so many stories that it just made sense to cluster them all together and create a concise, witty, and fantastic "how to be the woman in consulting that you want to be" guide.

Most consulting books are either truth tellers (uncovering a specific company's dirty laundry that didn't make it into the papers) or a persiflage on consulting (the exaggeration of small things, such as a consultant's behavior traits and things that are typical to the lifestyle). I have not come across a book yet that is fun to read, yet informative, and that also includes a bit of sass. So, I decided to write it.

So, what's the tea you ask?

Well, let me tell you . . . turn the page.

XOXO
Tanja, the original #girlconsultant

PART 1:

THE BASICS

CHAPTER 1

Why Consulting Is a Great Choice (No, Really . . .)

Welcome to chapter one. In this chapter, we'll dedicate some time here on why you should go for it. When you walk away from this chapter, you'll know why consulting is a great choice.

I'll also share with you one piece of advice a managing director gave me early on in my career (I think you'll find it quite useful) and address the vast amount of experience you can gain by being in this industry. Plus, we will dive into the fame you will take with you when you leave consulting—assuming you do leave at some point.

Lastly, we will talk about how books and pop culture portray consulting, and I will tell you what it is *actually* like. It's that whole "perception versus reality" thing. You know the saying "the glass is half full"? This is exactly what we will look at. We will look at the positive sides of consulting and how these benefit you, long-term.

Let's dive in!

So, why is consulting such a great career choice?

#1: Finding friends, learning people skills, and experiencing different leadership styles.

Whatever you do in consulting, you will always be with people. Everywhere, you will meet cool people, charismatic people, nerdy people, outgoing people, your kind of people, and sometimes not your kind of people. You will work with project managers, CEOs, and sometimes blue collar people from the client side. From your own company, you will work with young, smart, and driven people. These team members may keep changing depending on the project, but it will be fun, because the variety of people you work with will a) teach you people skills; b) develop your leadership skills; and c) give you more opportunity to choose your friends.

Project and team changes allow you to see and experience many different leadership styles. You will work for managers or consultants or even managing directors, and every one of them will be different. This is the beauty of it: If you absolutely love to work with someone, you can stick to them and look up to them as who you want to be when you grow up, or you can say "NEXT!" and switch to a different project and work with someone else. Project lengths vary from three months to over a year, so leaving one project and moving onto the next is not a big thing. In a more traditional nine-to-five job, switching bosses and departments willy-nilly is very difficult. You will be stuck with a boss for years and have nothing to compare it to.

All the Bosses

I have seen it all. No, really, I have. I have seen the choleric boss, the super chill boss, the narcissistic boss, the control freak boss, the we-are-best-friends boss, the assertive boss, and the list goes on. This is a true blessing for me because a) nothing surprises me anymore and I know how to work with any kind of boss; and b) I really know who I am and who I want to be. Observing and working under so many different types of managers and team leaders helped me discover the leadership style I use when I am in a position to do so.

While working on this book, I had a discussion with my boss (this was in a non-consulting position). She was trying to push me to be more controlling and to micromanage more, but this is absolutely not my style, and this is not who I want to be as a leader. I told her exactly that. I told her I aspire to be someone who people want to work with, and that upon distribution of tasks, people are so invested in the project that they will do everything to help and support. She was shocked by my very assertive and calm response. I left the discussion there. Afterward, I thought how thankful I was to have had all the prior experiences during my consulting career, to recognize how much I had evolved, and to be able to have that conversation and be firm on who I am and who I want to be.

#2: If you make friends, you make them for life.

Being friends at work is debatable. Some people come to work and are ever so professional. They would never open up to someone, because they have a separate life at work from their life outside of office hours. The only issue is that in reality, we spend so many more days at work than we do with family and friends, so it's inevitable that work and leisure will overlap at some point. There are other people who make friends with everyone. Sometimes they reveal too many details about themselves, which can then be used against them if these details land with the wrong people.

The golden middle—from my experience—is always the best. Two to four people whom you trust and are super-excited to see is a very good start.

I used to love asking the managing directors I worked with if there was one piece of advice they would share with me. One managing director told me: "Make friends that last, because as you grow and change careers, you can help each other out later in life."

#girlconsultant life hacks:

"Make friends that last, because as you grow and change careers, you can help each other out later in life."

I loved this piece of wisdom, and I really tried to make friends. Some friends stay, and others don't—that is just the nature of life. But it can be easy to grow together if you are together at work. All. The. Time. I still have about five or six friends who I know from my time in consulting. Even though I don't see them that often, we do chat from time to time and update each other on where we are in life. I know what they are up to and where they are currently working. I have also gotten job offers at the companies they worked for because they referred me internally. In fact, my current job was via internal referrals. I also know that if I ever need business advice, they would come and support me. It is comforting to know that if the sh** hits the fan, professionally or personally, there are people who would come through to help.

However, taking and asking too much from your network, especially from people you do not know too well, can backfire. Always try to be mindful about asking a favor of someone that you don't know too well. How would it make you feel if you were in their shoes? Also, don't be shy to say no to a request from your network if you don't feel comfortable or think it's inappropriate.

Consulting Girlfriends for the Win

I met some of my dearest girlfriends in consulting. They are ambitious, smart, and fun. I met Manja on an extracurricular assignment. Manja was setting up a fun Germany-wide video broadcast about the news of our industry practice for the company we were working for. It was broadcast once a month, and it was a change from the monotone monthly roundtable calls. Two managing directors who led the practice would show up and give us a rundown of the key performance indicators (KPIs) and the current "state of the nation." They would inform us about changes that were currently happening.

I was always looking for something creative, and upon announcement of the project, I immediately sent Manja an email saying I wanted to be part of it. We collaborated on this, and I got to know her better. We became friends and started hanging out after work, and we always asked each other for advice. Even now that we don't work together anymore, we are still friends. She is one of the wisest people I know, and every time we meet, I am inspired to be a better version of myself, and vice versa. Don't you want to meet your new bestie? She's out there waiting for you—maybe in the land of consulting.

#3: In the future, you will thrive in other professions.

At the beginning of your career, it might not be so simple to understand the benefits of consulting. You'll learn a lot of new things, meet a lot of new people . . . Anything at the beginning of something brand new can be exciting but also stressful. It can be difficult to see ahead when you're focused on what's right in front of you. So, I would like you to imagine yourself a couple of years from now.

Picture this: You are two years into consulting. You are feeling confident, experienced, and powerful, like you can solve any problem given to you. You are well-skilled in project management, Excel, PowerPoint, public speaking, communication and collaboration, people management, leadership, and, of course, your soft skills have grown rapidly with the number of people you have worked with. You are ready for a promotion to lead your own projects from start to finish. This means you will be calling your team to tell them about the project. You will work out the deliverables, then delegate and deliver the tasks in front of the client. Although it has been a challenging two years, you feel like your career, your paycheck, and your progress are where they should be. You have grown as a person and as a professional and have gained insights into more companies than you ever thought you would.

What does all of this translate to? You have built a foundation for your future career. As such, you can do anything you want. You can stay in consulting or move to a different industry or company; there are opportunities galore. Life is good because the world is your oyster.

The World at My Fingertips

My first two years in consulting flew by. It seemed like I looked left, and then I looked right, and two years were over. From my perspective, I was really young when I started consulting. I was 25 years old when I wrapped up my second year. I was still a kid, in my eyes. However, I was a kid wearing a suit, and I looked dashing.

I also felt very powerful. I had accomplished a lot in terms of personal growth in those two years. At 25, my then-boss gave me a team of people to manage, and I became a project leader. For me, this was a huge step. I had the hard skills and most of the soft skills, and I was so proud. I never thought that I could, and would, become the person to lead a team of others. Yet, being thrown into cold water over and over again in those early days (figuratively, of course) made me realize I could do anything. The world felt like it was right at my fingertips.

#4: The "fame" will follow you and open doors.

Let's talk about fame. That word "fame" probably sounds weird to you. We are not talking about becoming a famous singer or an actor in a blockbuster movie. But as there is in the arts, there is also fame in business.

Let me give you an example: Have you ever been introduced to someone and then the second sentence that comes out of someone's mouth is: "Well, Sandra over here went to Harvard! Did you know?" Then immediately, we associate attributes and make assumptions: *She must be really clever. She must be a hard worker. She must earn a lot of money now.*

It is the same with consulting. People always introduce other consultants with: "Alyssa was in consulting for company XYZ; did you know?" Then we are immediately in awe. We put this person on a pedestal, and we keep their name in the back of our minds because *If I ever have a really hard question, I will ask Alyssa; she will know what to do or how to solve it.*

What I am saying is: By being in consulting you'll automatically be given more respect because people see you as someone with clout, reputability, and prestige. And this "fame" can often open doors to additional opportunities because you're oh-so-fancy with your experience in consulting.

Name Dropping to Close the Deal

I was working in sales for a big tech company. There was one customer I was trying to close a deal with, but to close the deal they asked for a business case. Their goal was to present the return on investment to their board of directors, to legitimize the purchase of the licenses I was trying to sell. As I did not have time to do the business case myself, I asked a colleague who was an ex-MBB (find out more in chapter two: MBB refers to a highly prestigious consulting company) for support. Her role in the company was to help with pricing strategies to close deals, making my request within her scope of work (more or less). With some convincing, she was available to support me and, therefore, support my client. In the meeting with the client, I presented my Ex-MBB colleague's profile. On the slide I wrote: "Ex-MBB consultant with expertise in your particular industry will support you with the business case." That's it. That's all I had to say about her, and the client was in awe. The business case was top notch of course, and I really trusted her with the numbers. I went over them with her, but I could not find anything to improve. Ex-consultants are just THAT good.

Needless to say, no matter what job you do afterward, your prior consulting experience can come into play either in helping you attain a new position or providing support to someone else if they need your expertise.

Pop culture and its myths about consulting

Pop culture makes fun of consulting, because it is just such a different kind of job compared to any other standard business job. Pop culture thinks consultants are overpaid and kind of unnecessary, which is not really true if you consider consulting has been around since the early nineteenth century. On social media, you will find a lot of memes and fun things to look at with the hashtag #consulting. They make fun of the workload, the sometimes irrational requests that come at the last minute to change something on a slide, or the "consulting lifestyle," flying all over the world to attend business meetings. You'll also find a lot of acronyms, the so-called "Bullshit Bingo" used in the consulting world (which you'll see at the end of part two). In literature, some consulting books are really dark, portraying a picture of a "boys' club" and "elbow culture," as in: everyone is trying to get ahead and is willing to step over dead people to get there. They also depict people making use of their strategic alliances within the company because everyone just wants more power, more money, and more influence. They poke fun at flying all over the world and the miles or points you earn for your favorite airline or on your hotel loyalty card, but none of it makes consultants happy. If you follow these "stories" all the way through, then in the end you will have no friends or partner to share your free flights and free hotels with because of your workload and the pressure that comes with the workload. In my eyes, this is more of a satire and an exaggeration of things. In the end, it always depends on how you, personally, manage your work and your life. Most people I know have managed their work-life balance well, so be mindful and take breathers and don't forget to relax in between.

Contrary to popular opinion of the culture in consulting, it is the same in every company that I have set foot in. I have not found consulting to be toxic or perpetuating an extreme elbow culture. And it is not entirely a boys' club anymore, because more and more women are entering consulting, as you soon will, hopefully!

I have experienced consulting in a different way. I experienced teamwork, support, great friends, fun situations, constant learning, improving, achieving milestones, being super comfortable with travel, boarding a plane as easily as taking a bus, managing stressful situations, and becoming the best version of myself. I am the proof that there is so, so, sooo much more to consulting than what pop culture tells you.

I am writing this book because I had such a great experience, even though it was sometimes tough. Yet the reason I am where I am today, and the reason that I can pick whatever job I like, is because I have such a solid base of skills acquired during consulting. The reason that I am so assertive and confident is because I have seen it all, and I have gained so much experience that no matter the situation, I know I can trust myself to find the best solution with the information that I have available.

What pop culture, books, and news articles tell you about consulting paints a grim picture. However, real life is different. The real benefit of consulting is working with different companies and different people, giving you so many insights that you would never get by working in any other field.

tl;dr

- No other job teaches you such a great amount of things in such a short amount of time.
- The friends you make at work will become lifelong companions, people who can help and support you with advice on business, career, and maybe even your personal life.
- The job makes you resilient, and because you will have experienced so many types of people and projects, you will be equipped to manage every kind of situation.
- The fame and prestige will always be there, just like with an Ivy League university. You will always be known as the person who was in consulting, which is a good thing.
- Pop culture, books, and the press sometimes tell you one side (negative side) of the story. I am here to tell the others, because I would never have gotten this far had it not been for consulting.

CHAPTER 2

What the *Eff Is Consulting?

N ow that you have heard why consulting is a great choice, let me back this up with some facts: what consulting actually is, where it originated, and how I came to hear of it and start my career. This chapter will also give you background on the most popular kinds of consulting (strategy and management), so that in the end it is up to you to form your own opinion on the discipline you will thrive in. We will eventually focus on consulting companies (chapter 3); however, we will not talk about internal consulting departments within companies.

First, if you don't mind me asking, I have some questions for you: Where have you heard of consulting? Was the information positive or negative? Did you see a big advertisement at the airport and wonder what that company does? Did your university have a consulting club? (I am really curious to know your answers to these questions. If you have a moment, snatch my info in the "About the Author" section at the back of this book and shoot me a line.)

This is how I heard about consulting: I was in Shanghai, China, doing my master's in international business, and was quite close to graduation. Everyone was talking about what they were or were not going to do after they graduated. A lot of people were motivated by money; they just wanted to earn a lot. This was especially true for the people earning an MBA. They came back to higher education after having worked for a while so they could get a better job with a higher-paying salary once they graduated.

I was sitting at Starbucks with my then-boyfriend, and we were speaking about our future jobs. He was going on about how he wanted to go into strategy consulting and then later switch to private equity because his main objective was to earn money. He really had it all planned out.

I had a more naïve view on things. I always thought that no matter what I did, if I worked hard, I would make money. I also gave him this big speech about how I did not want to go into consulting, because people who were in the "Consulting Club" at Uni took themselves too seriously. Basically, I didn't know anything about consulting except for the people in that particular club. I had also never really seen any advertisements for consulting firms, even though they existed. Also, my parents have very classic careers—a doctor and a judge—and they did not know any consultants or any people in management. So, by the time I decided to give consulting a try, I really didn't have a clue. (The rest of this story continues later in this chapter.)

What consulting is and where and when it started.

Business consultants and authors Larry Greiner and Robert Metzger define management consulting as an "advisory service contracted for and provided to organizations by specially trained and qualified persons" who objectively work with clients to identify, analyze, and recommend solutions for business problems, and who may also help implement the solutions.[1] *Oxford Dictionary of English* states: "Consulting is defined as giving expert advice to other professionals in exchange for compensation, emphasizing objectivity to the problem of a company."[2] Having an outside perspective and knowledge of industry best practices allows companies to see beyond their borders and focus on areas they may have overlooked to help them achieve their goals.

If you don't know, now you know:

Consulting is defined as giving expert advice to other professionals in exchange for a fee, with a focus on being objective toward a company's issue.

Consulting originated in the nineteenth century in the United States, primarily in the areas technical and engineering consulting. Soon the field of consulting expanded into finance, business strategy, and organization, and the market for consulting grew.

In the 1950s, consulting companies expanded to Europe and helped the economy regain momentum after World War II. Between 1980 and 1990, the consulting industry grew from a handful to around 30 firms. According to Statista,

[1] L. E. Greiner and R. O. Metzger, *Consulting to Management* (Englewood Cliffs, NJ: Prentice-Hall, 1983), 7.
[2] Stevenson, A. (Ed.), *Oxford Dictionary of English* (USA, Oxford University Press: 2010) https://www.oxfordlearnersdictionaries.com/definition/american_english/consultancy.

during the twenty-first century, the consulting industry has grown significantly and is now one of the more established sectors in the professional services industry. With approximately $100 to $300 billion in revenue, the consulting profession has six major domains: strategy, management, operations, financial advisory, and information technology (IT).[3] When combined, these services and offerings span over 200 industry and functional areas.

Before we hop into the details, I would like to introduce one of the most useful business concepts: the Strategy-Operations-Tactics (S-O-T) construct[4]. S-O-T provides a framework for understanding organizational leadership, dynamics, and management, as well as their interplay in achieving results. This triad of words, originally from the military, refers to the three levels of warfare, and in a military context, links national objectives to tactical actions. In other words: What do I have to do on a daily/monthly basis, to achieve my goal in a year?

The S-O-T framework also assists in generating the best possible alignment between the organization's overall strategy and the operational level plans that divide the strategy into manageable chunks. Then the institutional systems and processes are required for successful execution, as well as tactics, techniques, and procedures. Using this framework really helps us understand the difference between strategy consulting, the

---

[3] Statista, "Consulting industry worldwide - statistics & facts," Statista, March 21, 2024, https://www.statista.com/topics/8112/global-consulting-services-industry/#topicOverview.
[4] Günter Schmidt and Wilbert Wilhelm, "Strategic, Tactical and Operational Decisions in Multi-national Logistics Networks: A Review and Discussion of Modeling Issues," *International Journal of Production Research* 38, no. 7 (May 2000): 1501-1523. https://doi.org/10.1080/002075400188690.

If you don't know, now you know:

Strategy-Operations-Tactics (S-O-T): This term originally comes from the military and refers to the "three levels of warfare." In a military context, the S-O-T links national objectives to tactical actions.

strategic part of the framework, and management consulting, the tactical and operational part of the framework.

With that said, let's focus on these two most popular domains.

Strategy consulting:

Let's talk about strategy and what you would be doing as a strategy consultant. This is the S in the S-O-T concept. The field of strategy is vast and can fill a whole degree's worth of classes at university. But to give you a good understanding, here is a quick definition: A business strategy outlines the plan of action to achieve the vision, mission, and set objectives of a company and guides the decision-making processes to improve the company's financial stability in a competing market.[5]

---

[5] Michael Boyles, "What is business strategy & why is it important?" Harvard Business School Online – Business Insights, (October 20, 2022), https://online.hbs.edu/blog/post/what-is-business-strategy.

If you don't know, now you know:

A business strategy outlines the plan of action to achieve the vision, mission, and set objectives of a company and guides the decision-making processes to improve the company's financial stability in a competing market.

Strategy is a high-level endeavor and usually has little to do with getting your hands dirty. The timelines can cover multiple years (one to five years), and assumptions must be made to plan so far into the future. Strategy consultants help with defining a vision, mission, and long-term goals and then create plans on how to reach those goals. Any business, no matter the size, should have quantified goals that are in line with their company strategy.

Let's say you have a company in the fashion industry, specializing in handbags. You hire a strategy consultant to analyze the industry and give you a market overview. She will identify the niche of the most practical work bag and define a strategy around that with a potential outcome based on similar successful companies. She finds that a seasonal product launch of 4,000 bags at a price point of $450 has been especially successful. Then you, as the company owner, determine, with her help, the specific goal you want to set based on her strategy, such as:

- I will become the company that sells the most practical work bags in the world. [strategy]

- In my first year, we will launch a new bag four times, with a total of 4,000 bags for the year at a $450 per bag price, and I will sell out all of them. [KPI]

Next would come the operational and tactical part of how this goal can be achieved (which is usually a management consultant's role, as we'll discuss shortly):

- The four product launches will represent all four seasons via the color and functionality of the bag. [operational]

- To ensure we sell out, I will focus my branding around those seasons. This includes creating and posting daily content on all social media platforms, locating brand ambassadors, and creating smart ads to target the right audience. [tactical]

One key differentiator is that in strategy consulting, most client counterparts are CEOs, heads of departments, and, in general, important people with important titles who would then be important enough to know and take care of a specific company's or business unit's strategy. Because of the perceived importance of the people involved, strategy consultants are often also seen as important. This assumption of importance may go to some people's heads. In other words, many strategy consultants see themselves as the "crème de la crème" of all the consultants. However, importance actually depends on the person and, of course, the company you work for. I will tell you all the details of the different companies in chapter 3.

Management consulting:

Let's look at management consulting (also referred to as "business consulting"). This usually comes after the strategy is set, with the goal of implementing the strategy. This would be the "O" and "T" in the S-O-T framework and refers to "advisory and/or implementation services to the (senior) management of organizations with the aim of improving the effectiveness of their business strategy, organizational performance, and operational processes."[6]

If you don't know, now you know:

Management consulting (also known as business consulting) is defined as advisory and/or implementation services to the (senior) management of organizations with the aim of improving the effectiveness of their business strategy, organizational performance, and operational processes.

Management consultants are like Jeeps: all-terrain, all-rounders. They can find themselves in every area of the company, usually working primarily for senior management, and

---

[6] "Management Consulting," Consultancy.org, 1.1.2024, https://www.consultancy.org/consulting-industry/management-consulting.

in every industry. Due to the great diversity in industry and specialization, management consulting represents over half of the consulting industry.[7] The other half consists of all other areas of consulting, such as technology, strategy, operations, HR, etc.

The scope of work is not so tightly defined for a management consultant. You may be asked to advise on business matters from the strategy to the operational to the tactical. Using our fashion example above: A strategy consultant would define how many product drops a year should be made, when, and at what price range. A management consultant would help define and execute what needs to be done to sell out these four drops at that price. And there you have the differentiation between the strategy and the management consultant. In real life, the borders are not drawn so clearly, and you may work on everything because the project is staffed or sold that way.

Management consultants are more hands-on people, from what I have witnessed in terms of projects and people that I have met during my career. This is not an either/or question. Just because you chose management consulting doesn't mean you can't do strategy consulting or vice versa. If you are unsure of which type of consulting is really your thing, you can always try both. You are in charge of your career, and you have the power to do whatever you want.

You have an advantage that I did not have, because you now know the differences between strategy and management consulting. When I started, I did not really know what I was getting into. I sort of heard about it but did not really have a clear idea.

---

[7] "Management Consulting."

25

The Truth About How I Got into Consulting

I did my master's in China, and after coming back to Germany, my then-boyfriend and I started applying for jobs. He found a job quite quickly, as he had worked before his master's and had connections. Me, on the other hand, not so much. I had no connections, and I could also not ask my parents to hook me up. They are not that kind of people and they didn't know anyone in management, let alone in engineering or supply chain, which is what my degree was in.

I didn't know what I wanted to do. I knew I wanted to learn a lot, and I wanted a fast- moving environment. I wanted to grow as a person, becoming the woman I wanted to be, and I wanted to work with people who were driven and wanted to achieve something. I applied to a lot of "trainee" positions at large corporate companies all over Germany. I also applied to entry-level positions in logistics at companies that had production facilities in Germany. I got a couple of interviews here and there, but nothing really culminated in a job offer.

Honestly, there was always something the interviewers did not like about me. It was absurd, and I never really understood it: I was too young, or I spoke too many languages; I was too international, or I was too confident. People are funny, especially when they are hiring. Most people from average companies will want to hire someone who is less smart or equally as smart as them, because if they hire someone smarter, they fear this person will take over their job. These people might also have internal fears and issues that may stop them from progressing or hiring someone who they think is "overqualified." Maybe.

In contrast to that, there are those companies whose policy is to "raise the bar," which means that every new hire needs to be better than the last or average employee. The bar is then raised for every candidate that comes after them. This hiring policy is a means to hire candidates who contribute to the success of the company, bring in new ideas, and have the drive to change things. I didn't know it back then, but I just needed to find a company where I could raise the bar.

Sometimes, people in hiring positions do not know a lot about international degrees, and anything but the ordinary, standard vita is something they cannot grasp, because they have not lived abroad or have simply not hired a lot of international people. I remember this one lady interviewed me for an internship position for a large beauty company. I was 19 years old and in the midst of my bachelor's degree. She literally got mad at me, and she kept interrupting me and telling me to go on vacation and not be so ambitious. I thought, *What am I, a Witch?* I work really hard, but I also really live my life. I have partied, I have the most amazing friendships (that I curate), and I have always taken the time to look at the waves for hours whenever I am at the beach. I walked out completely deflated from that interview, but I told myself that it was not meant to be and that I wouldn't be happy there anyway.

Flash forward to after completing my master's. I was 22, I had been applying for jobs, traineeships, and internships for a couple of months, and I still hadn't gotten a job anywhere. I still was not so sure about consulting, but I was desperate, and I just really wanted to start working. I was browsing for internships. It was the foot-in-the-door technique, and I saw a consulting internship in logistics. I thought to myself: "Let's give it a try. The description definitely seems appealing."

So yes, my big speech on how I thought people in consulting took themselves too seriously was long forgotten, because how was I going to base a career decision on hearsay? It looked like it was a good career starter, so why not find out for myself?

My future internship supervisor called me two days later and asked me for an interview. It was a short interview. I introduced myself and answered the question: "Soooo, tell me about yourself." And I was asked if the internship scope sounded exciting to me. Obviously, I said yes. The interview went well, and I got the position. I even got paid for it. Now, it was the absolute minimum the law required, but it was enough to cover my living expenses. I started in consulting via an internship, and I think it was the best thing I could have done.

Why was consulting the right choice in the end? Because it gave me endless possibilities. I knew I wanted to do something with business, but I didn't know what exactly. I studied logistics, supply chain, and engineering, so I knew a lot of theory, but I didn't know exactly what people were doing on a daily basis. Consulting enabled me to work with people in the different departments of the supply chain, from forecasting to purchasing, to sales and operations, to production and to aftersales.

I was in an environment that helped me grow into the person that I am today. Everyone around me was just a little bit smarter than me, which made me want to become the best version of myself. It didn't discourage me, it fueled me—like a challenge. I wanted to be successful in the things that I did, and I wanted to at least show that I was as smart as everyone else.

#girlconsultant lifehacks:

Pick an environment in which you can grow and surround yourself with people who make you want to be the best version of yourself. Growing as a person means going outside your comfort zone, and that means discomfort. Embrace it.

Now, you'll see as you read on through these pages that things were not always easy and didn't turn out the way I originally hoped or intended. But growing as a person means going outside of your comfort zone and that means discomfort. As you read this book, I will share my highs and lows with you, because your career (in consulting or something else) is not a linear line; it is a squiggly one.

What you think your consulting journey will look like:

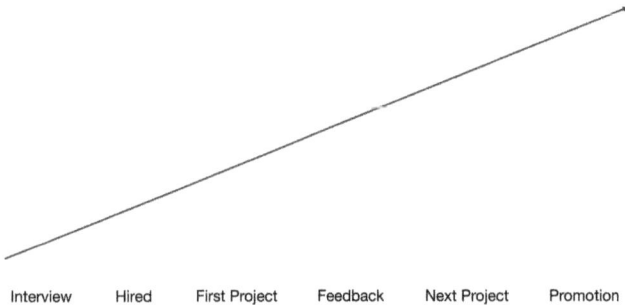

| Interview | Hired | First Project | Feedback | Next Project | Promotion |

What is actually looks like:

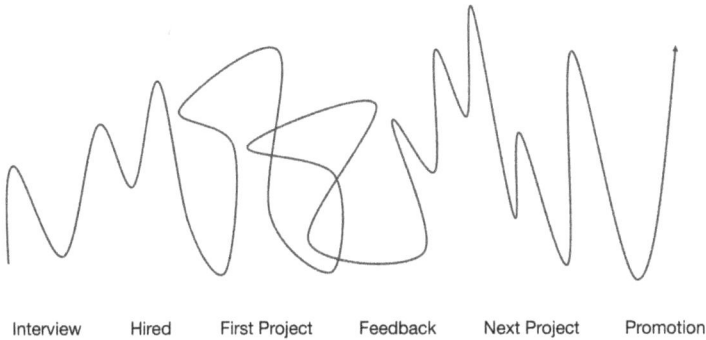

| Interview | Hired | First Project | Feedback | Next Project | Promotion |

tl;dr

- Consulting involves providing expert advice to professionals for a fee, focusing on objectivity and industry best practices.
- Consulting originated in the nineteenth century in the US, expanding to Europe in the 1950s and is growing significantly in the twenty-first century.
- The six major domains of consulting are strategy, management, operations, financial advisory, HR, and IT.
- Strategy consulting deals with high-level planning and long-term goals, while management consulting covers a diverse scope of work for improving business effectiveness.
- Starting with an internship in consulting offers valuable experience and opens up various career opportunities.
- A consulting career involves both highs and lows, requiring you to embrace challenges for growth.

31

CHAPTER 3

The Different Types
of Consulting Companies
You Should Know

There are a lot of different consulting companies out there, and if you zoom out far enough, they can be clustered into different categories. There are merits and demerits to each of these, and in this chapter, I will give you the pros and cons of each. Ultimately, I'm aiming to help you gain a good understanding of where to apply based on where you think you will thrive.

Before we get into it, here is a short questionnaire. Fill it out to see what type of company may best fit you.

POP QUIZ! Which Consulting Company Might Be Your Jam?

These 13 questions will help you determine whether you should consider working for a prestigious management consulting firm (MBB), one of the Big Four consulting firms, or a boutique consulting company. Don't worry, I cover each of these in the pages ahead. But since I don't want to skew your results by giving you the deets ahead of time, answer these questions as honestly as you can first.

1. What size firm appeals to you most?

   a. Large, prestigious firm with a global presence from 30,000 to 300,000+ employees.

   b. Smaller, more tight-knit team of 50 to 100 employees.

2. Are you looking for a well-established brand name on your resume?

   a. Yes, it's important for my career trajectory.

   b. Not necessarily; I value unique experiences.

3. Do you prefer a structured, well-defined career path and advancement opportunities?

   a. Yes, I want a clear career progression.

   b. No, I'm open to a more flexible career trajectory.

4. How important is work-life balance to you?

   a. I'm willing to work hard and long hours for career growth.

   b. It's important, and I'm willing to prioritize it.

5. Do you thrive in a competitive environment in which you are surrounded by top talent?

   a. Yes, I want to work with the best in the industry.

   b. I'm more focused on the quality of the work and team dynamics.

6. Are you looking for extensive training and development programs?

   a. Yes, I want structured training opportunities.

   b. I'm open to learning on the job and taking ownership of my development.

7. Are you interested in working with Fortune 500 companies and multinational clients?

   a. Yes, I'm drawn to high-profile clients.

   b. I'm more interested in working with a variety of clients, regardless of size.

8. How important is the potential for international assignments and travel to you?

   a. Very important; I want to work on a global scale.

   b. I'm open to travel but it is not my primary focus.

9. Do you value a more entrepreneurial work environment where you can have a direct impact on the company's direction?

   a. I'm more interested in executing established strategies.

   b. Yes, I want to shape the company's future.

10. How do you feel about the potential for bureaucratic processes in a larger firm?

    a. I'm comfortable with some level of bureaucracy.

    b. I prefer a more agile and streamlined approach.

11. Are you looking for a company with a vast network and resources?

    a. Yes, I want access to extensive resources.

    b. I'm more interested in a close-knit professional network.

12. Are you open to taking on a wide range of responsibilities, including client management and business development?

    a. I prefer a more specialized role with a focus on project delivery.

    b. Yes, I'm interested in a diverse role.

13. Are you motivated by the potential for rapid career progression and promotions?

    a. Yes, I'm highly motivated by career growth.

    b. I'm more focused on job satisfaction and meaningful work.

Tally your answers:

- If you have more "a" responses, you might lean toward pursuing a career with an MBB or one of the Big Four consulting firms. If you have more "b" responses, you might find a better fit in a boutique consulting company.

- Disclaimer: I have generalized here, to help build attributes to every category. However, companies may also differ from these typical clusters. In some Big Four firms, you can get paid for overtime, whereas in some boutique firms, working time can exceed 60 hours per week, and you aren't compensated for overtime hours. Large MBB's have offices all over the place, so they might not allow juniors to travel much as local staff may be available, while boutique consultancies do not have as many resources, so travel to provide staffing globally is crucial.

Now that you have your questionnaire results, you can pay closer attention to the consulting type you may be most interested in pursuing. So, allow me to give you the "tour" of consulting and how it breaks down into three different categories: MBB, The Big Four, and Boutique.

To be clear, in this chapter, we are not going to talk about internal consulting departments. Usually as a part of large corporations, internal consulting departments work on improving the processes and structures of the corporation and may report directly to the COO or CEO. We are talking about specific consulting firms who go into other people's corporations.

I need to mention one more thing before we get into it. There is one significant difference when it comes to consulting companies. Some are partner-owned, such as PwC, and the others are corporations, such as Accenture. Let me explain: Partner-owned means that partners buy into the company and own a part. Since they are responsible for the success of the company, they usually have their own business unit—a company within a company, so to say. They have their own clients and their own topic/industry, and they hire their own people. Every country is a separate entity; thus, cross-border engagements are also quite rare. In such a company, changing industries or topics/projects might also be more difficult. This company would be more for Option 2 girls (see chapter 4).

Then you have the corporation-like companies, in which only a few people run the country's legal entity in the respective country. The other partners receive their salary and annual bonuses. The partners have their departments, but they are more than happy to lend and borrow people from different departments and countries, because they are acting in the interest of the company as a whole. People who see themselves following Option 2 (see chapter 4) should ask the recruiter what kind of company they are applying to so they know what they are in for.

As we discuss, please bear in mind that the following points are based on my own observations and what I've garnered from reading books and surveying friends who have worked in the varying types of consulting companies.

MBB (McKinsey & Company, Boston Consulting Group, and Bain & Company)

The first category of consulting companies is the very well-known, very prestigious **MBB**, which stands for **M**cKinsey & Company, **B**oston Consulting Group, and **B**ain & Company. These are three separate American firms that were frequently clustered together as a reference to the largest strategy consulting (remember, we defined strategy consulting in the previous chapter) firms in the world, based on revenue. They made consulting popular amongst high achieving individuals, who aim for money and status. Due to their highly skilled employees and alumni network, their influence reaches far and wide across the globe.

If you don't know, now you know:

Definition: MBB refers to **M**cKinsey & Company, **B**oston Consulting Group, and **B**ain & Company, three of the most prestigious strategy consulting companies. They were clustered together into a single industry term due to their ranking as the highest in revenue.

A.T. Kearney Nowadays, their business model has largely shifted, and they are not just doing strategy work anymore but have diversified and offer a much broader portfolio of services. They are not always in the top 10 in revenue, yet their reputation and history precedes them. The term MBB is well-known and will probably not change in the future. They are a key player in the consulting landscape.

While the MBB category was coined to indicate the top three consulting companies, over the years, similar companies were founded in different parts of the world. Companies such as Kearney, L.E.K. Consulting, OC&C Strategy Consultants, Oliver Wyman, Roland Berger, Strategy&, and others can also be seen as part of this category (even though they are not the original MBB companies). If you want to apply to McKinsey, BCG, or Bain, then also know you can apply to these other MBB companies, too.

The main benefit of this type of consulting company is the branding and paycheck you acquire, and the main con is that it is very tough to get into.

Pros:

- The highest wages and bonuses in the industry.
- Yearly promotion rounds: most people stay two years; the ones who stay longer can reach the managing director level in five to seven years.
- International assignments and projects, meaning international travel and long haul flights involving a lot of flight miles and statuses collected to be used privately.
- Working for C-level clients—CEOs, CFOs, CTOs, COOs—which is very demanding but builds your network.
- Access to an external network of specialists available on-call to provide insights on any given topic.
- Large internal learning and knowledge platforms.
- A very steep learning curve, which is great for those who like a challenge and to continuously learn.
- Established processes and structure, which are the so-called best practices.
- Seniority-driven scope of responsibility and work; selling projects and acquiring new clients is typically only done at the senior and managing director levels. (In other words, when you start, you don't have to focus on bringing money into the company).
- Vast and powerful network of MBB alumni. There are many people in important positions, and they are always

willing to support and help anyone leaving the company for a job outside—the so-called outplacement. This is a win-win, because the company can sell more projects if its ex-employees are in decision-maker positions, and the ex-employees or alumni earn a lot of money and have a lot of responsibility when they leave MBB.

Cons:

- Long work hours; you are required to be on call most of the time (day and night).
- Up or out. If you don't get promoted in the required time set by the company, you need to leave.
- Heavy competition in terms of promotion (but not in terms of working together. Teamwork is taken very seriously, and they have a very helpful and supportive community.)
- High barriers for entry: You need to have excellent grades in math and ideally have graduated from a targeted university. Check for a list of target universities in your country. It makes it easier to get hired; however, it is not a must.

If you don't know, now you know:

A "target university" typically refers to a specific college or institution that is actively sought after by students, employers, or researchers due to its high academic reputation, strong programs, and notable achievements. It is a term used to denote a university that aligns with specific academic or career goals and is often a preferred choice for education, recruitment, or research endeavors.

MBB consulting would be a good fit if you really enjoyed strategy at university. You enjoy analyzing the market, calculating a business case, and giving suggestions on how to change a company's future.

Now, since we are becoming friends: as a friend, I believe I should tell you the truth. I want to empower you to make the right decisions. Here's the skinny . . .

I read a book called *When McKinsey Comes to Town*, written by investigative journalists Michael Forsyth and Walt Bogdanich from the New York Times.[8] According to the book, McKinsey advertises their positions to graduates as a chance for them to change the world. Many believe it and join, until they are asked to join projects which are straight up unethical. McKinsey's reputation hasn't been tarnished in the long run, and they are very powerful and have very good branding.

Honestly, I can't validate this from first-hand experience, but I felt responsible to share what I've read and to offer you some advice. If you ever become a McKinsey employee, you

---

[8] Walt Bogdanich and Michael Forsythe, *When McKinsey Comes to Town: The Hidden Influence of the World's Most Powerful Consulting Firm* (New York: Doubleday, 2022).

have the choice to say no to anything that doesn't fit with your values. (This is true with any employment opportunity.) Some people get weak and do things they should not do, especially if they fear saying no will result in not getting promoted or not getting requested for the next project. BUT, if you start working for McKinsey (or anywhere) and someone asks you to do something you don't think is ethical or that doesn't align with your values, walk away. No amount of money and prestige should make you spiral downward into depression because you cannot look at yourself in the mirror anymore.

The Big Four

The Big Four is the term for the four largest *accounting* firms by revenue: PricewaterhouseCoopers (PwC), Deloitte, Ernst & Young (EY), and KPMG. Each provides audit, tax, consulting, and financial advisory services to major corporations. Together with Accenture, which does not perform audits anymore (because of the big Enron scandal in 2001—see below), these are the largest accounting consulting companies in the industry. With diversified practices covering all areas of the business and offices around the world, they can cater to every customer because of a) their flexibility of onshore/offshore staffing; and b) their vast talent pools of people.

The above-mentioned scandal involved Enron Corporation, an American energy company, which engaged in widespread accounting fraud to hide its financial losses and inflate its profits. This led to the company's bankruptcy and the dissolution of Arthur Andersen, one of the five largest audit and accountancy partnerships in the world, which had certified Enron's accounts. Anderson Consulting was spun off from the accounting firm and was rebranded as Accenture. The scandal resulted in significant regulatory reforms, including the Sarbanes-Oxley Act of 2002, aimed at improving corporate governance and financial practices in the United States.[9]

> ## If you don't know, now you know:
>
> The Big Four usually refers to companies such as Deloitte, PwC, EY, and KPMG, which are the largest auditing and accounting firms worldwide in terms of revenue. Their high company headcount allowed these companies to expand their consulting portfolio and offer a large variety of services.

The main benefit of working within a Big Four company is the variety of things you can experience while being there. The con is that due to the size of the company, they maintain a large overhead of administrative people and you (as a consultant) do not get paid the big bucks.

Before I jump into my definition of pros and cons, I want to address that this list is not cut and dry. Depending on who

---

[9] Confidence Joel Ihenyen, PhD, Michael Ayakoroma, and Emomoemi Egiye, "Transparency, Accountability, and Investment Decision-making: the Case of Enron and Arthur Anderson," *EPRA International Journal of Economics, Business and Management Studies* (EBMS) 10, no. 9 (September 2023): 63-70 https://eprajournals.com/IJHS/article/11359/abstract.

you are, something listed can either be considered an advantage or disadvantage. For example, working within sales could be good or bad.

If you have more of an outgoing-type personality and like running the show, then sales might be something you will enjoy. This means you would write proposals, pitch to clients, and negotiate deals. It is definitely a really good school for fine-tuning your soft skills, which you will always need no matter where you are. Large companies usually have a separate sales department for big deals, and you are encouraged to support small deals at the consultant level (more on hierarchies in chapter 7). In smaller companies, there may not be enough people in general, so you'll have to support the partners in sales, or the sales may be done solely by the partners because they have the industry connections.

The other point which can either be positive or negative is the debate between specialist and generalist. This also depends what kind of person you are. Generally, in a high headcount company, there will be a specialist for everything. It's really just plain statistics: the more people you have, the more likely there is a specialist. This means that to differentiate yourself, you'll be encouraged to specialize. Contrary to that, if you work in a small company, being an all-arounder can help you build and support many areas of the business.

As you read, look at the list through your own lens. Which of these pros still feel like they would be beneficial to you and which cons would you agree are disadvantages? This list is merely my perspective. Apart from that, every other point can be classified as pro and con. Here we go:

Pros:

- Established processes.
- Internal wikis for knowledge sharing.
- Large internal learning platforms for additional certificates, specializations, etc.
- An expert for every topic within the company; just pick up the phone and call.
- More freedom to look around and try out different projects and topics.
- Larger teams and projects staffed with international people.
- No "up or out"; not getting promoted within the predefined timeframe is not a reason for termination.
- Good branding for your curriculum vitae (CV).
- Good work-life balance—some projects may be hectic; others not so much.

Cons:

- Lower wages than MBB (which means less money, but also less pressure).
- Working more for middle management in larger companies, because projects are generally more operational and hands-on. Usually only managing directors and senior members speak to top management, C-level executives.
- Hundreds of thousands of employees scattered in many different countries. The people turnover and the alumni network of the Big Four is more anonymous and scattered, because it is impossible to know everyone.

Boutique consulting

The third category, boutique consulting companies, includes every smaller consulting company that typically caters to a specific niche. Usually, a handful of managing directors actually own and work at the company. There are thousands of these companies, although mostly unknown by the masses. They can be very specialized and reputable in their own field.

If you don't know, now you know:

Boutique consulting firms are usually small- to medium-sized companies that offer their services in a specific niche to a more local client base.

The main benefit of working within a boutique consulting company is the velocity in gaining responsibility and moving up the ranks to earn more money and have a better sounding title. The con is the branding of such a company may not be so powerful, which means future employers may not be as familiar with these companies when they see them on your resume.

Pros:

- Lots of decision-making power without top management giving specific guidelines.

- A lack of standardized processes, meaning a lot of room for creating new ones. However, there is also a lot of room for discussion on how to tackle certain things.

- Likely to be more specialized, so if you are a specialist this may be a great fit.

- Quicker promotions (if the company's current financial situation allows for it).

- Higher wages and a good work-life balance as a means of attracting talent, since the name of the consultancy is usually not as well-known and is not as strong a brand as a Big Four firm.

- Few specialists in any particular area, meaning lots of opportunity to share your knowledge.

Cons:

- Not a great place to find a variety of industries and project topics as a generalist.

- Not much anonymity. If you don't get along with the client, or you don't like the topics you are working on, you might not be able to move to another project or client because there may not be many to switch to.

- Smaller internal repository of existing documentation and templates (both as slides and Excel formats), due to the limited number of people and topics in the company.

- Less rich internal learning platforms due to limited resources to set up and manage the contents.

#girlconsultant lifehacks:

"You can either be a small fish in a big pond, or you can be a big fish in a small pond. One is not better than the other, you just learn different things."
—My friend Renée

My Experience Inside a Big Four Consulting Company

After giving you a rundown of the advantages and disadvantages of every category, let me tell you about the company I worked for and why it really fit my strengths and personality. I worked for a Big Four company, and I could thrive in it, because a) I always need to be learning something new and I could change industries, projects, and teams as quickly as I wanted to. Yes, it was that simple. I would say that "this is not the industry that I want to work in long-term," and being interchangeable when fresh out of uni, it was easy to switch.

Of course, I could not "be the drama" all the time, because I had to also take care of my reputation, so I stayed on a project as long as they initially booked me for, and then if I didn't like it, I "rolled off" (i.e., I left the project); and b) I did not have to become a specialist. You can see this by how many times I switched industries and by how many projects I did (which you'll come to realize as you read on).

The Big Four consulting company life chose me, and I loved it. I was a small wheel in a big company, and I could move around and do projects as I pleased. At the beginning, I didn't know what I really wanted, and after studying engineering and supply chain, I wanted to try out as many projects as I could to find something that really sparked my interest. I started my career on a change management and communications project because I knew someone in that area and she staffed me on her project. I didn't have so much experience with change and communication, but I was ready to learn and fill the gaps, because let's be honest, a lot about change and communication is common sense, empathy, and logical thinking.

After six months, I had had enough of that, because at the beginning, the tasks were interesting, but then the client liked me and was looking for a task for me so that I would stay on the project. The only thing she had was to monitor the inbox of complaints that would be coming in due to the recent upgrade of the IT system. I was thinking: *I did not suffer through math class at university to be answering support emails.* Thus, I wanted to move, so I started asking around for something to do in supply chain.

I found something on a more strategic project, in which we were merging the purchasing departments together into one team, including merging them physically into one building. The company had grown over the years into silos, and purchasing ordered everything separately for their own brick and mortar stores. We had the task to save costs and basically re-engineer the department. It was exciting to see such a cost cutting endeavor in real life; however, most of the interesting work had already been done and I was more or less just executing someone else's thoughts, which was also fine for the time being. At least I had minimum responsibility and didn't have to work on something I had little understanding of or experience in.

Later, I moved to a transportation outsourcing project, where we carved out the whole transportation department and went through the process of hiring multiple large third- and fourth-party logistics providers to take over different segments of the worldwide operations. This project was unlucky staffing because I did not get along with my manager. He was (and probably still is) a narcissist. Even after multiple rounds of feedback, from me to him, to tell him what I needed in terms of leadership, it still was not possible to get good guidance. I left the project after four months and immediately got staffed onto the next project. New team, new manager, new client. It was amazing to change and to start fresh and to be successful.

Finally, this time I was on a really good project, and I could really kick some butt. I also liked the area I worked in, which was production planning and Lean Six Sigma operations. Something about seeing a product coming from a block of metal, moving through the production, and then seeing how it turns into a part that you later see built into an airplane was fascinating to me.

There were many more projects to come after, but at the beginning of my Big Four career, it was a rollercoaster. Yet the fact that I worked for a huge company allowed me to switch teams, projects, and clients quickly. If I wanted to explore an area, I could. I even went from management consulting to strategy consulting and back. I led my first project team after two and a half years in the company, and I was given a lot of responsibility.

Being in a Big Four was a great start to my career. I absolutely loved the variety and the possibility, and

I could live my "generalist" dreams. I could move from topic to topic, industry to industry. I was in the so-called "pool" at the beginning, because I wanted to see and learn everything, before (more or less) building a track record and sticking to one industry and topic.

I got to really explore, learn, and look around. I could only do that because I was at a Big Four company. My main objective to go into consulting was to learn. I wanted to find out what I liked, and I wanted to improve my current skills and learn new skills. I wanted to test my boundaries and push myself to see what I was capable of.

I'm telling you this story because I think it's important to find a company that will be a good match for who you are as a person and how you work. After having read through all the pros and cons of the types of companies, in which one could you see yourself?

Ultimately, it is up to you to know yourself and to know what is important to you. Do you want to earn money? Or do you want to learn? Or do you want to have your freedom to see as many projects and as many people as possible? I think all consulting companies are fun to be in and in the end, if you don't like one, then just switch and go to the next.

tl;dr

- There are different categories of consulting companies: MBB, the Big Four, and boutique consulting firms.

- MBB firms offer prestige, high wages, and fast promotions but may have long working hours and intense competition for promotions.

- The Big Four provide diverse projects and international opportunities, but wages may be lower, and specialization might become necessary.

- Boutique consulting firms offer decision-making power and quick promotions but may lack variety and established processes.

- It is essential to consider personal strengths and career goals when choosing the right consulting company.

CHAPTER 4

Two Paths to Building Your Consulting Career

L et's assume, shall we, that you've decided you're going to give consulting a shot. You know the reasons why consulting can be a great gig, and you know the types of companies you could work for. But don't stop there. Have you considered what happens once you get in? As in, what direction will you go? Do you want to be a generalist and know a lot of things quite well, or a specialist who knows one thing on another—more excellent—level? Do you want to make an entire career out of consulting, or get your feet wet and then move on?

In this chapter, I want to give you an outlook on how your consulting gig can fit into your long-term plan. I am a fan of knowing what the options are, and I am here to present you with two (this is a non-exhaustive list). There isn't just one way of doing things, and you may wish to carve your own path. Remember to take the power into your own hands and make the decisions you think are right for you. It's okay if you don't know the answer to this right now. It's also possible for your answers to change over time once you get your foot in the door. Give a thought to these next two questions:

1. Are you interested in consulting to find out what topics, industries, and projects interest you and what you want to work on later in life?

2. Are you in consulting to get promoted, make a lot of money, travel places, and live a life of prestige and reputability?

Let's look at each option a little more closely:

Option 1: Consulting is just a stepping stone.

At uni, we study theory, but how do we ever know what an actual job looks like in any field, regardless of how hard we've studied? Like anything, the way to learn is by doing. So, the way you find out about consulting is to get a job in consulting, try out as many projects in different areas as you can, and work for as many clients as you can. When (and if) you have found your passion (which hopefully you do), then you can stay and gain more experience in that field, and eventually you can leave the consulting world to pursue your career in something dedicated to that area of interest. Of course, you don't have to get specific or become THE specialist. You can continue to explore a variety of areas and stick to the generalist's path.

That said, being a generalist or bouncing from project to project is not the best strategy to get promoted quickly. Continuously changing teams means working with a lot of people and always having to prove yourself and your skills over and over again. You may vibe with some people and with others you won't—such is life.

According to my experience, many people look out for their own interests and are eyeing you to determine if you are useful to them or not. For example, a manager is more likely to push and support you during a promotion round if they're able to determine they'll benefit from you in the long run. For example, if they get promoted, can they give you more responsibility if you continue working for them? No one should be looking at you solely as something to be taken advantage of to help them gain, but as you'll come to find out in a later chapter, sometimes you have to play the politics game and form strategic alliances even with those who are trying to get ahead. After all, trying to get ahead isn't necessarily a bad thing, it's just about how you go about it. But I digress . . .

Choosing to project-hop or remain a generalist does not mean that you will NEVER get promoted. I was shopping around on different projects, and I also still got promoted. You just have to be smart about the kind of brand you build for yourself and the people you connect with. Now don't despair. In chapter 11, I will tell you how to do that. Just note that brand-building is not the only thing that will help you get promoted. You also have to work hard, take on responsibility, and prove you are ready for the next step.

So, to recap: In this option (using consulting as a career stepping stone), you would get what you want in terms of insights into different industries, projects, and clients, but you would have to invest more time into brand-building and stakeholder management to increase your chance of getting promoted.

Without Knowing, I Chose Option 1

Now that you know me better, I'm sure you can guess that I am a generalist. Maybe you even assumed that because I am trained as an engineer, and yet I wrote this book; these are two very different things. The truth is, I have a lot of different interests, and I like learning new things to see if I like them or not.

I studied supply chain, which, if examined closely, consists of various subparts: long- and short-term planning, sourcing, supplier management, customer management, production planning, transportation, purchasing, after-sales, etc. When I came from university, I did not know which of these departments I should apply to, because I was afraid I was going to start in one, it would be full of repetitive tasks, and I would be unmotivated and eventually fall into extreme boredom. Nevertheless, I applied to several open positions. But when the question came in the interview: "Why do you want to work in this department?" my answer was never really convincing. How should I have answered that question, if I didn't know what I would be doing in that job? *Repetitive tasks excite me?* Come on. *eye roll*

You can imagine how thrilled I was when, after I got into consulting, they told me I could choose where I wanted to belong, or I could be in the "pool," which meant no specific orientation, no industry affiliation, free to go on whatever project came next. I loved that! And I managed to get exactly what I needed at that time. I needed to contribute to projects in all different areas to find the one I was mostly interested in, which turned out to be production. Yes, your girl had her security boots under the table, and she wore them with her dress. Production satisfied my need as a creator—the need for seeing the raw material getting turned into the final product. I was looking for an area where I could see the progress being made.

I wouldn't have discovered that had it not been for the access I had to so many different areas of the field. I got to spend a lot of time with different project groups, and although I did not vibe with everyone, it was a great experience, because I got to work with all types of people, thereby giving me vast knowledge and understanding of people's behaviors. Because of this varied work experience with a variety of people, nothing really surprises me anymore. This enables me to keep calm in most situations. I even know how to manage my bosses, depending on who they are, as a result of all I have learned. Choosing to start as a generalist and use consulting to explore a field of interest worked out really great for me.

Option 2: You are in it to win it.

Depending on where you are in life, you may need different things, and financial security is part of that. Consulting can be a great choice when it comes to financial security or monetary gain. There's a lot of money that can be made here. Yet apart from the monetary gain, people stay in consulting because they really LOVE their jobs. (Or they are insecure overachievers who are in it for the prestige and fame, and their personality profile keeps them in the race, because their self-worth is tied to their work.)

But if right now you are looking at going into consulting to get promoted and to earn more money, then great. You have different moves you can make. For instance, if you get really laser-focused on one area and specialize, you can become known for something specific and that draws the right people's attention—the people with the power to promote you—especially if you are good at what you do and the people you have worked with speak highly of you.

How soon you get promoted and start earning the big bucks probably depends on what career stage you start in consulting. If you're starting out early in your career, perhaps with no spouse or children, you might be able to put in more time and energy to your career development and get noticed more quickly, therefore rising through the ranks faster. If you are a more seasoned or mature professional by the time you begin consulting, you might already have the confidence, assertiveness, and networking skills (I cover all three in this book, so be on the lookout) to develop your own personal brand, which helps you with those strategic alliances that inevitably get you noticed and get you promoted.

In consulting, as in any other company, you need a sponsor and advocate—someone who believes in YOU. I believe in you, but I cannot get you promoted, unfortunately. This person is someone who trusts you and who believes in your "charisma, uniqueness, nerve, and talent," (as RuPaul of *RuPaul's Drag Race* would say) and, of course, your ability to deliver the tasks. The more you work with a boss who really likes you, the more she will want to see you win. She wants to see you get promoted, grow, and take on more responsibility.

#girlconsultant lifehacks:

Getting promoted requires finding someone who trusts you and who believes in your "charisma, uniqueness, nerve and talent," (as RuPaul of *RuPaul's Drag Race* would say), and, of course, your ability to deliver the tasks.

Naturally, if you have found a boss and a team you vibe with, but the topic you are working on is not so thrilling, you can excel at it anyway. And if a promotion is important to you, then my recommendation is to stick to that team, make yourself stand out, and work your way up. Staying longer will help you gain trust. Trust is one major part of the promotion process, but you also have to deliver value and perform at the next level. Performing at the next level also means engaging in sales activities—selling more projects. If you build up a great reputation with your client and get to expand your network at the client site, you are more likely to sell more projects. With more responsibility and more money, in the blink of an eye (okay, it might take some years, but time passes really quickly in consulting) you will be a managing director, earning goodness knows what. All I know is I hear *cha-ching* in your future.

tl;dr

- When considering a career in consulting, think about your long-term goals and how consulting fits into your overall plan.

- There are two main approaches to consulting:
  - Option 1: Using consulting as a stepping stone to gain exposure to various industries and projects to find your passion, while knowing that continuous team and project changes may slow down promotions.

  - Option 2: Pursuing promotions and financial success by building trust with colleagues and senior-level staff, as well as engaging in sales activities to sell more projects.

- Ultimately, prioritize your personal values and goals when deciding how to approach your consulting career. What matters most is finding the right path for your individual growth and happiness.

PART 2

INTERVIEWING AND GETTING HIRED

CHAPTER 5

Getting Your Game Face On for the Interview

N ow, dear #girlconsultant, let's talk about the interview process. If you are going to give consulting a go, you will want to know how to get through the interview.

Interviews in general can be intimidating, and consulting interviews are a little different from regular ones. In chapter 6, we will go through the different parts of the interview. In preparation, I'm using this chapter to share six things I wish I understood earlier, so you are set up for interview success before you even arrive.

In this chapter, we will cover:

1. What it means to be professional in an interview
2. My favorite breathing technique to calm my nerves
3. Attentive listening and relevant question-asking
4. Assessing whether a job is the right fit
5. Accepting rejection
6. How to stay as authentic as you can

Now let's put our big girl panties on, because if I can do it, so can you. Let's go!

The pep talk

What would you do if you were not afraid?

This question changed my life. I read these words when Sheryl Sandberg's book *Lean In* came out, and she is absolutely right. "What are we afraid of?"[10] As women, growing up, we are constantly criticized for being too smart or not smart enough, being too fat or too thin, being too short or too tall, or wearing too much or not enough make-up. There is always someone who has an opinion. So why are we so afraid to show up exactly the way we are? Why do we want to be liked so much that we bend back and forth and try to make it right for everyone?

When you walk into the interviews, do not be afraid of the people with whom you are interviewing. Obviously, their role is to judge you, but do not pretend to be someone you are not, and do not be afraid of rejection. As we are approaching the part of the book where you will learn about the consulting interview, I am here to motivate you and prep you the best I can.

If you are in your 20s, this is the time to try things out, grow as a person, and push the boundaries of your comfort zone so when you reach your 30s, you can proudly say that you like the woman you have become, have reached a level of income that you are happy with, and stay calm in most situations, because you have seen and experienced so much already.

6 pro tips and tricks from my consulting interviews

I've been to a lot of interviews in my career. With all that experience, I know a thing or two about interviews. But I have

---

[10] Sheryl Sandberg and Nell Scovell, *Lean In: Women, Work, and the Will to Lead* (New York: Knopf Doubleday Publishing Group, 2013), 12.

condensed this knowledge down to my top six tips, which I am handing to you here. Consider dog-earing this page or high-lighting or underlining these tips. You do you, Boo.

Be professional

An interview is basically an opportunity for you to show your future employer how professional you are. Before we speak about being professional, I am not going to lie; it took me a long time to understand what "being professional" actually means. A quick internet search produces the definition: Professional conduct involves being thoughtful, formal, and dedicated. While the standards of professionalism can differ across industries and individual companies, maintaining a professional demeanor ensures that you are seen as trustworthy and dependable.[11]

For me, being professional is about conveying trust. They say trust can only be built over time, and the interview is a time when you lay the first ground stones of trust, such as being on time. The interviewer and you have taken time out of your day to have this conversation, so being on time is nonnegotiable. Trust can also be conveyed if you have researched the company, the interviewer, and the role in advance to build common ground.

Next, dressing for the part is key, because when people judge you, the first thing they see is the way you are dressed. If you have put effort into being well-groomed and dressed nicely (e.g., a suit is recommended), then the interviewer thinks you put effort into all the work that you do (or at least that you know when to make an effort). They are also going to watch

---

[11] Jennifer Herrity, "What Does It Mean To Be Professional?" Indeed, March 10, 2023, https://www.indeed.com/career-advice/career-development/what-does-it-mean-to-be-professional.

the way you represent yourself by how you respond to questions or listen when they're talking. Your interviewer is looking for clues as to how you might be when you meet clients, facilitate workshops, or build long-term relationships.

#girlconsultant lifehacks: 3 Tips to Displaying Professionalism

- Be yourself; do not try to be someone you are not.
- Convey trust by being on time and dressing appropriately.
- Embrace your unique traits and show your personality, to help build a connection with the interviewer.

Fight those nerves

Many of us have experienced nervousness at some point, a phenomenon deeply rooted in the intricate workings of our body's response to stress. It begins when the brain perceives a threat, activating the hypothalamus, which then signals the pituitary gland. This chain reaction culminates in the adrenal gland, located above the kidneys, releasing adrenaline, which is a stress hormone. You've likely felt its effects: a racing heart, dilated pupils, and increased blood flow to your muscles. These responses are part of the "fight or flight" response, a survival mechanism that dates back to our earliest ancestors.[12]

However, the response is not uniform; its intensity varies based on the perceived threat and the importance we attach to the situation. For example, a job interview, while not life-threatening, can trigger this biological reaction. This occurs because adrenaline diverts blood from the digestive system to more critical body parts, a process essential for quick response, primarily the skeletal muscles and the brain but resulting in less critical systems, like digestion, temporarily shutting down.[13]

It's important to note that while the fight or flight response has been a vital survival tool, it can be maladaptive in modern times where threats are less about physical danger and more about psychological stress. Chronic activation of this response can lead to long-term health issues, such as cardiovascular disease. This historical survival mechanism highlights how our bodies' ancient responses are sometimes mismatched with contemporary stressors.[14]

So how can we deal with nervousness? One effective technique is the use of mental imagery. This method is popular in the world of sports, and it involves athletes mentally rehearsing a specific skill before competing or training. It might

[12] John M. Grohol, PsyD, "What's the Purpose of the Fight or Flight Response?" *World of Psychology Blog*, December 4, 2012, https://web.archive.org/web/20130323170934/http://psychcentral.com/blog/archives/2012/12/04/whats-the-purpose-of-the-fight-or-flight-response/.
[13] Neil Schneiderman, Gail Ironson, and Scott D. Siegel, "Stress and health: psychological, behavioral, and biological determinants," *Annual Review of Clinical Psychology*, no. 1 (2005): 607-28, https://www.ncbi.nlm.nih.gov/pmc/articles/PMC2568977/.
[14] "Biopsychology: The 'Fight or Flight' Response – Evaluation," Tutor2u, March 22, 2021, https://www.tutor2u.net/psychology/reference/biopsychology-the-fight-or-flight-response-evaluation.

sound unconventional, but this practice actually stimulates the relevant parts of the brain associated with that skill. Before your interview, you can imagine what it would be like to sign the contract, and what your first day on the job would look like. By imagining yourself with the end result you want, you are focused on positive thoughts before the interview, which can improve your confidence that you are the right person for the position. So, the next time you feel those nerves kicking in, consider trying techniques used by Olympians and other athletes. It might just help you perform at your best. Ready, set, go!

World: 100, Me: 0. How My Nerves Kept Taking My Interviews

I had just gotten laid off from my fashion job, which had to skim down on personnel because the COVID-19 pandemic had forced them to only keep core business relevant people. As innovations manager, I did not belong to that group. In such a time of uncertainty, I was looking for a new position. No one knew how long the pandemic was going to last, and no one knew what was going to happen. I also didn't know where I wanted to go— if I wanted to go back to consulting or continue

working in the industry. All I knew was I was failing every single interview. I remember the feedback
I got from one company was that I came across like
a sociopath, because I nervously laughed at something that was sad. I also had to do the interview in
German, but after speaking English for most of my
life, it was really hard to find the right words during
a stressful situation to express myself correctly.

Basically, I was nervous in every single interview. I
did not eat or sleep properly. I really thought there
was something wrong with me. I felt stuck, so I
decided I needed to book a session with a career
coach—someone who would help me understand
why I was nervous during these interviews and coming across that way. I knew this lady from a woman's
network I was in, and I had won a group coaching
session several years back with her. Back then, I
learned quite a bit from her, and I felt really confident that she could help me. I came prepared with
So. Many. Questions. She gave me a lot of technical
advice, but the one thing I left with was confidence
in my abilities and a breathing technique that really
helps in stressful situations, which I share with you
below. It relaxes you instantly and clears your head.
The recommendation is to do this for two minutes
every day for one week leading up to the interview,
or make it part of your morning routine with medi-
tation, journaling, etc. Now I do not usually journal

or meditate, even though I probably should start. I just did this breathing technique the week before the interview. The moral of this story: It is okay to be nervous, but get some support to help you calm those nerves so you can perform better in interviews. Otherwise, no one can see how capable you are and how much you might shine in their company.

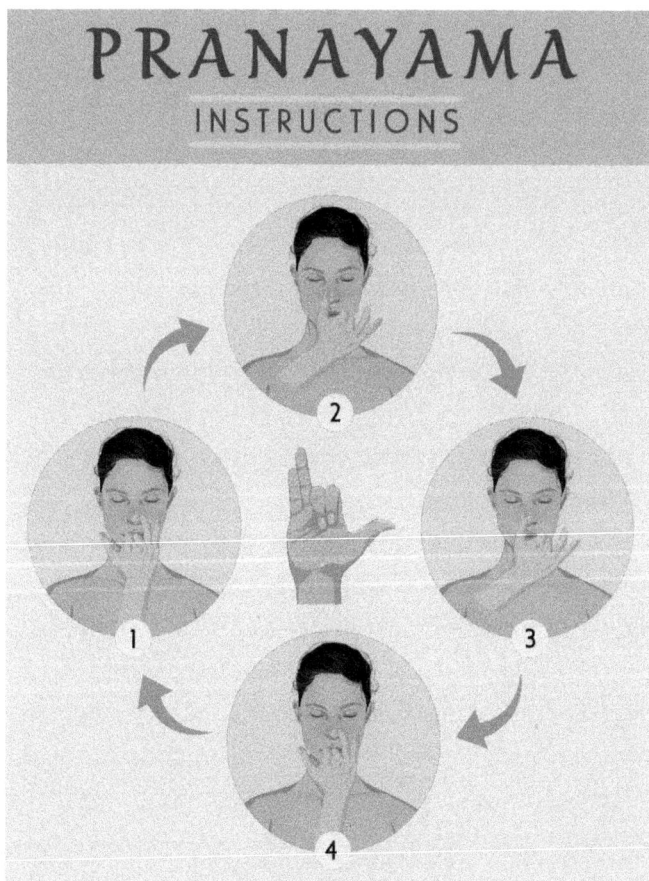

PRANAYAMA
INSTRUCTIONS

Calm your nerves with pranayama: Interviews can be nerve-wracking, but there is a simple breathing technique described in Hindu texts which is used in yoga that can help you relax. Place your index and middle finger on your forehead, in between your eyebrows, and alternate closing each nostril while breathing. This technique can be practiced daily and for about two to five minutes before interviews.

#girlconsultant lifehacks: 3 Tips to Fight Those Nerves

1. Try mental imagery and focus on the result you want.
2. Breathe deeply.
3. Be confident and assertive.

Listen attentively to your interviewer (and ask relevant questions).

An interview can be a stressful situation, and you may be really focused on yourself. "Am I sitting straight enough? Can she see my sweaty fingers? Is my hair out of my face?" With all that focus on you, it can be difficult to really listen. Whenever you catch yourself, just remember you are FABULOUS, and then get back to paying attention! So, get in there and listen to what questions the interviewer really asks you.

To prove you have been attentively listening, you can summarize what your counterpart said to mirror that you understood. "So, if I understand correctly . . ." You can also ask follow-up questions after they have finished speaking, starting with: "That sounds interesting. May I ask a question?" This is more eloquent than jumping in and saying: "Sorry for interrupting, but . . ." Because, you know, #sorrynotsorry.

I had been to a couple of interviews and was so worried about myself that I did not listen. And this became clear to the interviewer when we came to the part when they asked: "Do you have any questions?" I did, and I got them talking about their favorite project ever. They spoke for at least three minutes, but rather than paying attention, I was more focused on what I was going to ask next. So, when they stopped talking, instead of appreciating their story, or showing interest, I asked a completely unrelated question, which of course drew the attention back to me (and the fact that I was not listening). It was something like: "Do you think that the languages that I speak will help me in this job?" I mean, seriously. Could I have been any WORSE in having a conversation? They looked confused and irritated. I would have, too, in their position. So, do not be like me. Listen and ask relevant questions.

#girlconsultant lifehacks: 3 Tips for Active Listening

1. Keep eye contact and focus on listening and understanding the questions asked.
2. Summarize the interviewer's points to show that you comprehend what is being discussed.
3. Ask relevant follow-up questions to demonstrate your interest and engagement.

If you don't know, now you know: Questions You Can Ask During the Interview

When I was interviewing for roles, I always thought it was difficult to ask good questions, because a) I did not want to ask too many questions about the role, out of fear of looking like I did not know what I was applying for; and b) because I did not know what was important for me at the workplace, so I did not know what specific questions to ask. BUT, since I am here to help you, I have included some things you *could* ask. I have left more space on the page for you to add your own questions. As you think of these questions, really ask yourself what is important for you in the workplace, and then try to come up with questions that would get you more information about those aspects of the job or company. Tailor your questions to what matters most to you.

A great time to ask questions (aside from when they ask you if you have any) is at the end of the interview when they are done asking you their questions. This is the time to assess whether the company is the right fit for you and inquire about the company culture, leadership style, performance measurement, and project types. Try to also ask questions that are not based on the job description (i.e., what is the background of the open position: is it because the company is growing, or is it backfill [i.e., did anyone leave the company, and why?]).

- How would you describe the culture of the company, and can you give some examples?
- If you could change something about the company/your job, what would it be?

- How would you describe the feedback culture; for instance, is it customary to have weekly or bi-weekly one-on-ones with one's boss?

- How would you describe your leadership style?

- How is performance measured?

- How would you describe a typical week of yours?

- How would you describe the impact that you have?

- What kind of projects will I be working on?

- What is the general leadership style?

Add your own questions here:

_____

_____

_____

_____

_____

_____

_____

_____

_____

_____

_____

_____

_____

_____

It needs to be the right fit.

Knowing if a job is the right fit is a particularly difficult thing to assess, because whenever we apply for a job, we have read the job description, and we can really imagine working for that company, right? We make up all these scenarios in our head—what it would be like to walk into their headquarters; would we need to move to another city; what housing we would need to find, etc. The more emotionally involved we get—which is good, because companies want you to want to come and work for them—the more difficult it is to see red flags. Plus, when we don't get the job, the disappointment is high.

I have been to interviews where I walked in and knew the person sitting in front of me was a dick. With one company, it was my second interview, and the guy was explaining everything again, just in more detail—information that had already been explained to me in the first interview. He told me, in a very condescending way, how the first interview was not relevant. That should have been my first red flag—discrediting the work of his colleague. The next red flag was that as soon as I spoke, he interrupted me and spoke over me. The third red flag was when I asked him about the promotion process of the company, and he said it was solely his decision, because he was head of HR. At that moment I should have said, "Thank you very much for your time, but I think I do not want to work here." And I should have shaken his hand, stood up, and left.

I did not, because as always, hope dies last. That said, I was not surprised when I got a rejection. Yet, I also felt a level of relief because the amount of politics inside that job would have been a real burden if I got it.

Maintaining objectivity in job interviews, recognizing red flags, and staying true to your authentic self is essential to ensure a good fit with the company culture and increase your chances of finding a more suitable job elsewhere if needed. If you do not get along, or if you think the company culture is weird, then you are probably not going to be happy there. Stay authentic and true to what you know you want and value in a workplace, because you will find a better job somewhere else.

#girlconsultant lifehacks: 3 Tips for Knowing if It's the Right Fit

1. Listen to your gut; you need to feel good in the interview.
2. Spot the red flags and trust them.
3. Consider the alternatives; you do not have to want every job.

Accept rejection, release and let go

Most of us girls want to be liked. That means, we do NOT want to be rejected. Am I right? Well, here is the surprising thing! Everyone gets rejected. And I mean EVERYONE. The beauty of interviews is that you can get better the more you practice.

#girlconsultant lifehacks: Practice Makes Perfect (even with interviews)

Rejection is a natural part of life, and everyone faces it. It is not a reflection of your worth. Stay resilient and learn from each experience. Rejections can lead you to better opportunities that appreciate your unique abilities. Consider the number of successful people who were rejected repeatedly before striking it big. Here are some examples:

- When Bill Gates was looking for someone to invest in the original version of Microsoft, he pitched his program to 100 investors, and the 101st investor agreed to give him money.

- J.K. Rowling spent six years working on her first book as an unemployed single mother who was living on government benefits. Her own publisher rejected her dream, saying it was impossible for her to support herself writing children's books! Twelve publishers turned down her book before it was finally accepted by Bloomsbury. Now she is worth over $1 billion.

- Oprah Winfrey was born in 1954 and had to overcome much hardship and rejection in her early life because she was a Black woman. Finally, she became a co-anchor on Baltimore's WJZ-TV but got fired from this dream job. But what happened next? She went on to set up her own show and is now a self-made billionaire.[15]

In society, we think that as soon as we are rejected, we are worthless and we will never amount to anything, because that is what we have been told growing up. It is important to not take the rejection personally, because in general, if you have prepared, studied the company, practiced, and shown up as your best self, rejection is not a reflection of you; sometimes it is about not having the right fit or exactly the right blend of skills, or it is about being overqualified. Sometimes the positions that you have applied for are also just "alibi" job postings, and the position has been filled with an internal candidate. I also nearly did not get a job because the people on the panel thought I was overqualified. Just imagine, I got a rejection, and I would dig a hole for myself and question my abilities. Then you need to take your *charisma, nerve, and talent* and go to a different company that appreciates you.

---

[15] E. Jay, "Do the rich and famous really work harder?" *The Literary Review* 39, no. 3 (1996): 352-354.

#girlconsultant lifehacks: 3 Tips for Handling Rejection

1. Remember, everyone gets rejected.
2. Practice your answers beforehand and go to as many interviews as you can.
3. Feel confident at all times. If you did not get the job, it does not mean anything is wrong with you; it means something better is out there.

Try to be as authentic as you can

Being authentic is a difficult endeavor because we also want to appear "professional" and strive to fit in within a company culture. Still, it is important to weave things into the interview that make you, you. You would not want to come across one way in the interview and then show up on your first day and confuse them into thinking they have hired someone else entirely.

Wear the jewelry you always wear—the rings, the necklaces. If you do your hair or makeup in a certain way, keep it. If you are a cheery person, smile, or if you have a loud laugh or voice, laugh loudly and speak loudly. Or if you have a quiet, composed voice, keep that. Embrace your authenticity during interviews. Be conscious of the occasion, of course, but dress and act like yourself, including your sense of style and personality traits. I had a badass colleague who rocked a nose ring and wore a small black skull ring, but then she also wore a dark blue suit, and a pair of sneakers to look the part. You get the gist? This is the kind of juxtaposition I am talking about. Being genuine will help you find a workplace that aligns with your values and fosters a positive working environment. You need to feel comfortable with the people you will work with. After all, you will spend at least 40 hours of your week with them.

One of my most authentic traits is that if someone makes a good joke, I laugh loudly and wholeheartedly. Even in an interview setting, I laugh exactly the same way I always laugh. The latter convinced my recent hiring manager to hire me because she felt good vibes and she thought that if she hired me, we would have fun working together. This confidence only came about in recent years though. When I was in my 20s, I tried to look like everyone else. Little makeup, no jewelry, hair tied to the back, shirt tucked in. I was told those were the "rules" back then. Now, I show up dressed for the part (I have always worn a suit and love suits) and wear all my makeup and a lot of jewelry and do my hair the way I usually wear it. That is to say, so much has changed when it comes to bringing yourself to work, and as you gain more confidence in who you are, you will be more willing to show up as *you,* even during the interview stage. But if you can, embrace the idea of showing up authentically even now. Even when no one knows you . . . yet.

Stay authentic!

#girlconsultant lifehacks: 3 Tips for Being Authentic in the Interview

1. Wear the jewelry, makeup, and hair as you usually do.
2. Laugh at the joke.
3. Do not dim your light.

tl;dr

- Be professional but authentic in interviews. Show trustworthiness by being punctual and dressing appropriately, while also letting your unique personality shine.
- Calm your nerves with imagery exercises or breathing techniques.
- Practice active listening during interviews. Summarize the interviewer's points to show understanding, and ask follow-up questions to demonstrate engagement.
- Ask meaningful questions at the end of the interview to assess whether the company is the right fit for you.
- Embrace rejection as a natural part of life. Learn from each experience and stay resilient in your job search.
- Stay true to yourself in interviews. Embrace your personal style, behavior, and traits, as it is essential to find a workplace that aligns with your values.

CHAPTER 6

The Four Parts of the Consulting Interview

T he consulting interview is not your average interview. There are four parts to it, versus the average interview's one part, which is usually entirely centered around your personal motivation. You know the question: "Tell me about yourself and why you want to work for us." Those traditional, standard interviews are about you sharing past work experiences and situations when you demonstrated leadership, teamwork, and resilience and, of course, leveraged your hard skills.

In consulting, you have the personal motivation part, AND you will probably need to complete a case study and an estimation case. "Brain teasers" are not always on the agenda, so make sure to ask the HR person to provide you with the details for the day ahead of time so you can prepare. For the sake of completeness, I will talk about brain teasers in this chapter so you know what to expect for those interviews that include that portion. Since this book is not supposed to be a complete consulting interview prep guide, (business frameworks can fill whole semesters at university), I will explain what it is and its purpose, provide an example, and share some resources for materials to help you practice.

The interview parts may come across as a little overwhelming at first, but remember: If they have invited you to an assessment or a series of interviews, and you have passed the formal requirements, that is a good sign they want to hire you. The interview is a time for you to confirm this is true and to make a positive first impression. So be confident! I know you can do this!

Here's something else to always remember. Practice makes perfect. This includes interviews. Preparing for interviews (of any kind) increases your chance of getting the job.

#girlconsultant lifehacks:

Practice makes perfect. This includes interviews. Preparing for interviews (of any kind) increases your chance of getting the job.

A Memorable Consulting Interview

I have had many interviews over the years, and the one that got me my consulting job was quite memorable. You might recall that I used the foot-in-the-door technique to get into consulting by doing an internship. Usually, there are multiple steps to the interview process to land a job in consulting. The first one is with HR, via the phone, focusing mostly on your personal motivation. When you pass that round, the next step is a full day on-site with multiple rounds of interviews, with a partner or a manager. In this part, you go through the personal motivation, the case study, the estimation case, and perhaps the brain teaser (which we are going to cover momentarily because I know you are going to get past that first measly phone interview.) Because I did an internship, I got to skip the first HR interview, but I still had to show up for the full day of interviews. Back in the day, we even got invited to a dinner the day before. This is how the whole thing went down.

The night before

I looked at my watch; it was 7 p.m., and I was just getting ready to go for dinner. The full day of interviews took place in my hometown in Düsseldorf, Germany, but instead of going back home for the night, I chose to stay in a hotel with the others. It was closer to the interview venue.

Dinner was at 8 p.m. (which is the normal time to have dinner in Germany), in quite a fancy bar and restaurant. I made my way to the restaurant because I didn't want to be late. I wore my dark blue chinos and a blouse with a casual blazer. I love chinos, they are way more comfortable than jeans.

Upon arrival, the interviewers and HR personnel were already there. Other candidates were just coming in and making themselves comfortable. There were at least 10 people in total. I chose a seat and sat down, and I noticed there were wine bottles on the table. We were allowed to pick whatever we wanted from the menu, and of course, I did not pick the most expensive thing, but I never do that when someone else is paying.

I politely conversed with my seat neighbors and had the occasional sip of wine, making sure to just have one glass. I thought it was a test. They wanted to see if I could act normal at dinner and not get absolutely wasted on free booze!

After dinner, people started to stand up, and walk around the table to converse and introduce themselves to others they were not sitting next to. I am usually not the kind of person who likes that, but I took all my self-confidence and walked around the table to introduce myself to the HR staff. I shook their hand and we spoke about the weather and the lovely food, and how beautiful the location was. You know, the usual small talk.

We had a nice chat, and once the bill was paid, everyone began getting ready to leave. I also made my way back to the hotel with the others. After all, the next whole-day interview process started at 8:30 a.m.

The morning of

It was only a five-minute walk from the hotel to the office where the full day of interviews would take place, and since I am more on the late side in the morning, I had breakfast in a rush, got dressed quickly, and arrived at the office by 8:20.

I wore a suit, a dark blue one, with a white blouse, tucked in, and I was wearing flats. I was already sweating through my blouse by the time I arrived, but thankfully I was wearing a blazer . . .

The itinerary of the day was handed to me. I had just enough time to glance at it and to drop my bag, and off I went to the first interview.

Let's stop this tale here, as I want to point out some useful tips from this portion of my interview story . . . to be continued.

#girlconsultant lifehacks: For the Night Before and Morning of the Interview

Do:

- Pick out your outfit the night before.
- Make sure everything is ironed.
- Dress in layers.
- Pack deodorant in your purse.
- Do your breathing exercises from chapter 5.

Don't:

- Let them see you sweat.
- Don't wake up late and rush through breakfast and then arrive all out of breath and late.
- Get wasted on the free wine at the dinner before and wake up with a hangover.

Personal motivation

The personal motivation part is for the interviewer to get to know you and for you to get to know the interviewer. It is also for you both to see if the vibe is right, and if you can picture yourself working there. The interviewer will check your qualifications, and you should check if you can imagine yourself doing the tasks that are expected of you.

> ## If you don't know, now you know:
> The personal motivation part is for the interviewer to get to know you and for you to get to know the interviewer.

When I was younger, I always dreaded the question of what motivated me to apply for the job, because I always thought: "I am applying to this company because I need money to live, thus I need a job. Please give me a job." Without having any references from previous employers, and without knowing what I wanted to do in life, this was a hard question.

Usually, the personal motivation question begins with the interviewer crossing her legs on the other side of the table, adjusting her glasses, and saying: "Now tell me about yourself."

This is the part where you tell your story. Who are you, where did you study, what did you study, and why? What are your hobbies, what were your extracurricular activities at university? The next big question the interviewer will likely ask you is: "So, why do you want to go into consulting?"

Of course, the first thing you answer is, "I read this fabulous book called #girlconsultant, which inspired me to go into this profession!" *wink, wink*

But in all seriousness, the reasons for going into consulting include: A steep learning curve, seeing different industries and working on different topics, and working with a lot of talented and motivated people. I do not want to put words in your mouth, but these are good reasons to go into consulting, and they will be ones that delight interviewers to hear. Find your own way to say these or choose the ones that feel right. I am not encouraging you to lie if you do not believe there are good reasons for going into consulting (and if that is the case, you probably would not be interviewing) or if these are not the ones you would choose.

Back to the story—The Personal Motivation Question

My full day of interviews was packed; every minute was planned out. I was picked first to go and do my personal motivation portion. As I walked into the interview room, there were two people in front of me smiling. The day had just started when already they tried to crack a joke. I laughed politely: "Hahaha." *Let's get on with it*, I thought to myself.

Of course, it was all about who I am, where I come from, and why I wanted to join consulting. My answer is, of course, well-rehearsed and on point, and I mentioned the following: because I wanted a steep learning curve, I wanted to work on interesting projects, and I wanted colleagues who are driven, with a can-do attitude. I also referenced my internship, which I absolutely loved. My supervisor was someone who really cared about developing his people. I really, really looked up to him. They seemed happy with this answer, and then proceeded to ask me more about myself, such as what I studied and why, and tried to understand if I could be useful to them in their current projects.

I had a very "vanilla" feeling during the interview. The two of them were constantly looking at each other. Maybe they had something going on? Who knows. I thought I did a pretty decent job and left the room.

Stay tuned! There's more to come.

#girlconsultant lifehacks: For the Personal Motivation Interview

Do:

- Practice, because practice makes perfect, and in a stressful situation, it will be easier to look back on the things that you have learned.

- Focus on your achievements: what was the situation, complication, and solution, what you learned from those experiences, and how they can help you in your consulting job.
- Keep calm and do not let the interviewers distract you with comments and looks.

Don't:

- Panic and sell yourself short (you are amazing; shine bright).
- Forget why you want to go into consulting.
- Skip over asking the right questions at the end of the personal motivation part.

Practice makes perfect—personal motivation

I know it is a lot of work, but I strongly recommend practicing this personal motivation part. Set up your phone in front of you, with the camera in selfie mode so you are in focus. Place the phone in a way that you see yourself, although this may be distracting. If that is the case or if you would rather not watch yourself during your practice run, then use the rear camera of your phone. Record your pitch and then watch it back until it does not hurt to watch it anymore. Repeat this as many times as needed until you are happy with your pitch.

Also, wear the clothes you would wear during the interview because we behave differently depending on what clothes we wear. Then hit the record button and sit down. Answer the following questions:

- Tell me about yourself. Who are you?
- I have read your CV. Tell me some things that are not on the CV.
- Can you tell me about a time when you were successful at work?
- Can you tell me about a time when you failed and how you managed that?
- Why do you want to work here?

The two parts—tell me about yourself and why do you want this job—are the perfect parts to practice. You can practice in front of the camera, by yourself in your room, or record an audio file. How do you come across? Would you hire yourself? Did you mention all your achievements?

When I recorded myself for the first time, I was shocked. First, I noticed such a huge difference when I was talking about myself in German compared to in English. I leave out half of the things when I speak in German, because I just cannot find the right words on the spot. This is because in theory I am German, but I grew up abroad and studied and worked in English, which back in the day made it hard for me to express myself in German. I realized that I was not highlighting my achievements enough when I spoke in German. I would just mention them in one sentence, instead of elaborating and giving a clear picture. Lastly, since I cannot sit still, ever, I was fidgeting around with my hands, and that made me look very nervous. So, I practiced again and again until I was happy with my performance.

> ### Pro Tips and Resources:
> Watch the TED Talk "Fake It Till You Make It" by Amy Cuddy. It covers how to build confidence through believing in yourself.

The case study

The case study method was first introduced in the field of law in the late nineteenth and early twentieth centuries. Law schools began using real-life cases to teach students how to analyze legal issues, apply relevant laws, and develop arguments.

In the early twentieth century, business schools, notably Harvard Business School (HBS), started using case studies as a teaching method. In 1921, HBS faculty members began writing detailed accounts of real business situations, and students were asked to analyze and propose solutions to the problems presented in these cases. The method became popular for its focus on practical problem-solving and decision-making skills[16].

As management consulting firms began to establish themselves in the mid-twentieth century, they recognized the value of the case study method in training their consultants. Consulting firms saw case studies as a way to simulate real-life

---

[16] Todd Bridgman, Stephen Cummings, and John Ballard, "What the Case Study Method Really Teaches," *Harvard Business Review*, December 21, 2021, https://hbr.org/2021/12/what-the-case-study-method-really-teaches.

business challenges and develop their consultants' ability to address complex problems faced by clients.

Nowadays, consulting companies use the case study to assess a candidate's ability to solve a real-life issue in a structured way. The approach is conversational, meaning you ask questions at the beginning and then you tell the interviewer the steps you would take to find a solution. In the end, it is not so important that the numbers calculated are correct; it is more important that the way you came to your solution was structured and clear. What is key is your ability to guide the listener through your approach to solve an issue. It is easiest if you use business frameworks to guide your answer. A framework in consulting is a structured and systematic tool used to analyze, assess, and understand various aspects of a business or industry. It helps you organize and understand complex business situations, make informed decisions, and develop effective strategies. (There is an example of one called "Porter's Five Forces" in a few more pages.)

If you don't know, now you know:

A framework in consulting is a structured and systematic tool used to analyze, assess, and understand various aspects of a business or industry. It helps you organize and understand complex business situations, make informed decisions, and develop effective strategies.

There are a lot of different case study questions. Some are more strategic and others are more operational. The interviewer will probably pick a case study from the department and industry she is in.

If you apply to a small consulting company specializing in pricing strategies, most probably you will have a case study that includes creating a pricing strategy. If you are applying to a larger consulting company, the questions you get may be less predictable, since the interviewer can be from any part of the company. She may be in Oil and Gas and ask you a supply chain question, whereas a different interviewer may ask you about a new market entry. In the latter situation, it may be best to have practiced a diverse set of questions and business frameworks, have a broad understanding of the different topics, and not sweat it. You can ask questions during the interview and just think logically about the topic. Not to worry here, girlfriend. I've got you covered.

Responding to the case study question

The answer to a case study question is one part quantitative and one part qualitative. In the qualitative part, the solution is best described in a structured way. You always have a pen and paper in the interview. Use it and draw little sketches of what you are talking about, like you would on a whiteboard.

If you don't know, now you know:

The answer to a case study question is one part quantitative and one part qualitative. In the qualitative part, the solution is best described in a structured way.

First, summarize the issue the client is facing: "Did I understand it correctly? [insert rephrasing of the scenario]." If you did not understand the issue or the question, then clarify it at the beginning, or ask questions to clarify it.

Then proceed to organize your thoughts. You can say: "Can I take two minutes to organize my thoughts?"

Write down in keywords how you would solve the issue. Create buckets of things that you will analyze (e.g., the parties involved in the decision-making), or if you can use a framework, write down the different sections.

Narrate what you will do. For example, "To solve this question, I will discuss the following categories: price, promotion, product, and place." Then proceed with price, talking about the price of the product and what impact it has on the bottom and top line, or if it were to change, what other customers would it appeal to, and is the current customer base the right one? In this manner, go through the other three Ps, and draw a logical conclusion.

In most assessments, you will be asked to either take the numbers that are given to you to calculate (e.g., the feasibility), or you will have to guesstimate some numbers yourself. You can always ask the interviewer: "Do we have any data to support this issue?" Usually, the answer is yes, and they might even hand you a sheet of paper with some graphs. Which is great, because then you can really dive into the details, spot trends, and understand the influences of the solution.

Back to the Story—The Case Study

You can either be asked on the spot to discuss the case study, or you can be asked to prepare one. On my interview day, I had to prepare. I remember getting a stack of paper, with a case study that was three pages long, and it came with an additional three pages of see-through foil. I also spotted some pens to draw on these foils in the middle of the table. "Aha, I thought. So, this must be for the slides I am supposed to draw." I was right. With an additional seven pages of white sheets, and around one and a half hours to prepare, I went for it.

I remember the case study was about this family-owned beer brewing company whose CEO had always sold a steady product portfolio. Her name was Beenish (I know you imagined the CEO being a man. He probably was in the original case study, but we have more women CEOs now, too, so in my version, she will be female.) Her daughters wanted to make the company more sophisticated and introduce more variety. So, they opened bars and sold memorabilia. However, the costs were higher than expected, and the new products did not perform as expected.

The case study had financials attached and at least four graphs. It was my job to go through the financials and the sales graphs and to analyze which products the brewery should keep and which they should get rid of. Of course, there is a framework for everything, and the best-known and most classic one to take when it comes to product portfolio is "Porter's Five Forces."

I remembered there was no supervisor in the prep room, and I cheekily looked up and glanced at the framework on my phone, just to make sure that I remembered every part of it correctly. So, I thought I would scribble my thoughts onto the white sheet first, and then I would transfer the final version onto the foil. I was anticipating that I would have to present them on an overhead projector.

I looked at the financials, and I analyzed the worst performing product category. Then, I did a market analysis of the products I thought should stay, with the help of Porter's Five Forces. I also did a cost-and-profit diagram on another foil. I only had five minutes to present, so I thought two foils were enough.

When it was my turn, I went into the presentation room and saw a projector lined up in the middle facing a screen. *Aha, correct, the overhead projector it is.* I remembered these projectors from my school days, when we didn't have laptops and PowerPoint slides yet. I know, all you digital natives will not know anything about overhead projectors, but let your older sister tell you about it!

In the front of the room were three people staring at me, reminding me that I only had five minutes. This was on purpose, I later found out. They do this to make you even more nervous. That comment only motivated me to speak even faster. And so I did. I raced through my foils and finished in a whopping six minutes. Then they had follow-up questions, and in the end, we stayed 10 minutes.

In retrospect, I think I should have just taken 10 minutes in total, at a normal speaking pace. I think they just wanted to test how I reacted under extreme pressure. Back then, not very well. Nowadays, I would probably ask: "Is it okay if I take 10 minutes of your time? I would like to present all my findings because all of them are important." You know, the goal is to be assertive in these situations (more in chapter 8).

But hey, that is why I am here, to tell you that you can also challenge the recruiter.

To be continued . . .

If you don't know, now you know: Porter's Five Forces

Developed by Michael E. Porter, this framework is used to analyze the competitive forces within an industry. It helps consultants and businesses understand the attractiveness and profitability of an industry and the competitive dynamics at play.[17]

The five forces include:

- **Threat of new entrants:** Assesses the ease with which new competitors can enter the market and pose a threat to existing

[17] Michael Porter, "The Five Competitive Forces that Shape Strategy," *Harvard Business Review,* January 2008: 79-93.

businesses. Higher barriers to entry make the industry less attractive for new players.

- **Bargaining power of suppliers:** Examines the influence suppliers have over the industry in terms of pricing, quality, and availability of inputs. Strong supplier power can impact profitability.

- **Bargaining power of buyers**: Analyzes the power of customers to negotiate prices and terms. When buyers have significant power, it can put pressure on profitability.

- **Threat of substitute products or services**: Considers the extent to which alternative products or services outside the industry can meet the same needs. High availability of substitutes can limit a company's pricing power.

- **Rivalry among existing competitors:** Evaluates the intensity of competition within the industry. High rivalry can lead to price wars and reduced profitability.

#girlconsultant lifehacks: For the Case Study

Do:

- Practice your frameworks beforehand.
- Keep your eye on what you want to present at the end and work out the details for that.
- Talk your interviewer through the case study if it will be done without preparation.
- During prep: Take your phone, and check stuff if you are not sure about something.
- Leave time to draw your slides with the materials you are given.

Don't:

- Speak too fast and try to do everything they ask you to.
- Don't try to analyze everything; sometimes there are more graphs than you need just to throw you off.
- Don't be afraid to ask clarification questions.

Practice makes perfect—preparing for case studies before the interview

A case study is always going to be part of a consulting interview regardless of your level.

Practice makes perfect. So, practice, practice, practice. There are a lot of case studies online. You can even sign up on some websites and get a real practice buddy or a chatbot, with whom you will be able to practice the cases.

Also, practice math questions on paper, such as long division, large number multiplications, and percentage calculations, just to mention a few. There are easier ways to calculate large numbers in your head; if you have done the GMAT (Graduate Management Admission Test), you will probably know some of them. If you have not done the GMAT, then you should practice and look at some "how to do math in your head" videos online.

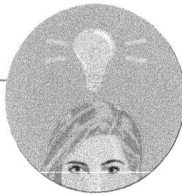

Pro Tips and Resources for Frameworks

The profitability framework is one of the most used frameworks. You can assess the profitability of a company or a product.

For example, the profit matrix:

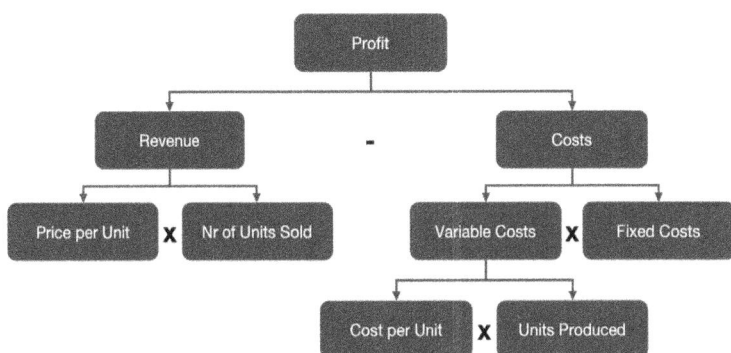

The estimation case

The estimation case, also known as the market sizing case, is a core part of a consultant's toolkit. The use of estimation cases in consulting interviews has a relatively long history, dating back several decades. However, the specific form and focus of estimation cases have evolved over time[18].

In the 1970s and 1980s, consulting firms began using estimation cases to test a candidate's mathematical skills and general business acumen. These cases often involved complex calculations and required candidates to demonstrate proficiency in statistical analysis and financial modeling.

In the 1990s and early 2000s, the focus of estimation cases shifted toward more strategic questions, such as market sizing and forecasting demand for new products or services. Consulting firms began to recognize the importance of not just

---

[18] My Consulting Coach. "Case Interview Preparation," My Consulting Coach, accessed August 24, 2024, https://www.myconsultingcoach.com/case-interview.

analyzing data but also understanding the broader business landscape and industry trends.

More recently, estimation cases have become even more focused on innovation and disruption, with many consulting firms seeking candidates who can think creatively and strategically to identify new business opportunities and navigate a rapidly changing business environment.

Despite these changes, the core purpose of estimation cases has remained the same: to evaluate a candidate's ability to think critically, break down complex problems into smaller components, and arrive at accurate and well-supported conclusions. Most consulting interviews require you to do an estimation case. It is a case to test your structured thinking and your advanced reasoning skills. It does not matter what the actual number is at the end; it is about being able to show how to get there by segmenting the question. Of course, the questions they ask in the interview may be quite boring, but, at least they are relatable.

Examples of Estimation Cases

1. How many taxis are there in New York?
2. How many electrical sockets are there in Germany?
3. How many nappies are sold in a year in France?
4. How many golf balls fit into an Airbus A320?

If you don't know, now you know:

The core purpose of estimation cases has remained the same: to evaluate a candidate's ability to think critically, break down complex problems into smaller components, and arrive at accurate and well-supported conclusions.

There are several steps you can take to tackle an estimation case in a consulting interview. The estimation case is to be solved through conversation. Walk the interviewer through the steps below, tell her what you are calculating and why, and what your assumptions are.

#girlconsultant lifehacks: Steps on How to Crack an Estimation Case

1. **Clarify the question:** Make sure you understand the specific question you are being asked and what information you are expected to

provide. Ask any necessary clarifying questions to ensure you fully understand the problem at hand.

2. **Identify the key variables:** Determine the key variables that will affect the estimation, such as the population size, market share, or average price point.

3. **Make assumptions:** Based on the information provided, make any necessary assumptions about the market or industry in question. These assumptions should be reasonable and logical. To make decisions, you have to be comfortable with the unknown, because in the real world, you can never know everything.

4. **Break the problem down into smaller parts:** Break down the estimation problem into smaller, more manageable components. This will make the problem easier to solve and help you identify any potential areas of uncertainty.

5. **Apply a structured approach:** Use a structured approach to solve the problem with the help of business frameworks. This will help ensure that you cover all the necessary components of the estimation and avoid missing any key variables.

6. **Check your work:** Once you have arrived at your estimate, double-check your work to

ensure that your calculations are accurate and your assumptions are reasonable.

7. **Summarize your results:** Since the interviewer has been following your train of thought, she can easily understand how you calculated your answer. In the end, clearly summarize your estimate, including any assumptions or limitations, to the interviewer in a clear and concise manner.

Depending on where you live, you should know the population in that country. The questions are usually tailored to the country or even city you are in to make them more relatable. Some may also ask you more difficult questions, as in example four from the list I provided earlier ("How many golf balls fit into an Airbus A320?"), so I recommend you go over some volume formulas. In this case, you would calculate the volume of the different parts of the aircraft and the volume of a golf ball, and then divide one by the other. Of course, you can also add the packing efficiency of spheres formula, see how you get along with time, and add it at the end.

If you take the second example ("How many electrical sockets are there in Germany?"), you would start by saying:

There are two categories in this question. First, there are the electrical sockets where people live, and second, the electrical sockets of the businesses around Germany.

At the end of the interview question, you should have the below diagram on your piece of paper in front of you:

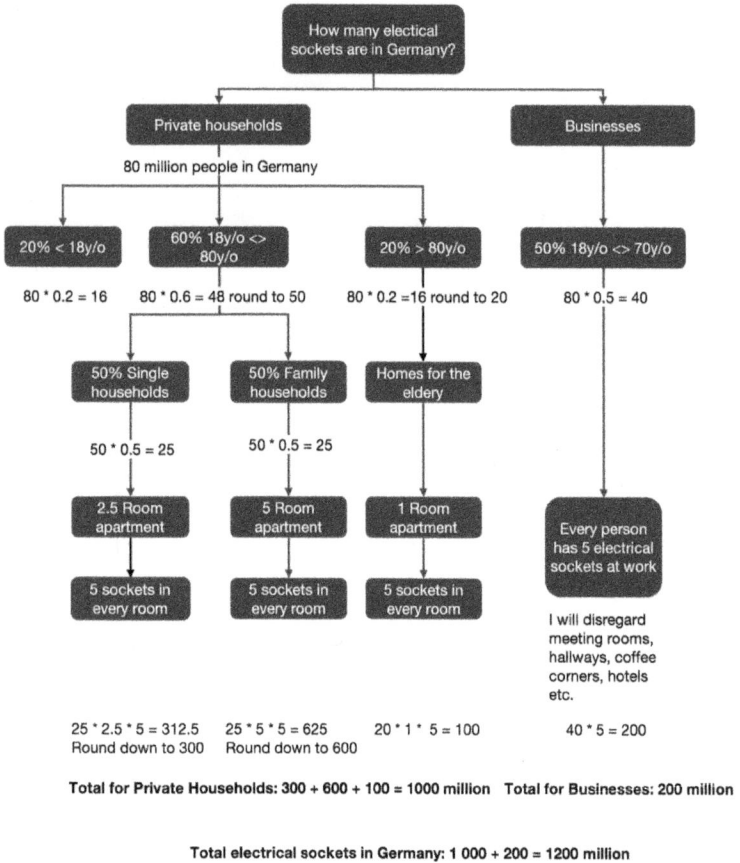

While going through it, narrate every step:

First, I will categorize the question into two buckets: private households and then businesses.

Let's start with private households, I would cluster the German population into three different groups:

Kids and babies, older people, and everyone in between.

We don't need to consider kids and babies anymore, because they live with their parents.

Then we cluster the adults and the people above 80 years old. (20 percent of older people, because we have an aging population in Germany).

That leaves us with 50 million people between the ages of 18 and 80, who, with a probable 50/50 split, are either single or have a family.

Assuming the single people live in a 2.5-room apartment with a total of five electrical sockets per room.

Assuming that two people live in the family household of a five-room apartment, with five electrical sockets per room.

And assuming that 20 million people live in elderly homes or single-room apartments, with five sockets in total.

We conclude that the total for private households is 1,000 million electrical sockets.

For businesses, we can assume that half of the population goes to work and that every employee has at least five electrical sockets either in her office or where she works.

We conclude that there are 200 million electrical sockets in businesses.

Leading us to a total of 1,200 million sockets in Germany at a specific point in time.

As you may have noticed, we made a lot of assumptions, which may not reflect 100 percent of the reality, but that doesn't matter, because this exercise is about simplifying the numbers so that you can calculate them in your head (or on paper via long multiplication/division) and come to a final number.

The estimation case is part of the interview because this type of situation can happen once you are on the job. For example, you would be using this market sizing framework if you had a conversation with the CEO of a company, you're throwing growth ideas around, and then the CEO asked you: "So what if we added natural cosmetics to our product portfolio?" Then, as a good consultant, you would say: "Well, let me estimate the market size for that in [country xyz]." Then you do the estimation case and end up with a number. Then the CEO would reply: "So how much money would that make me?" and you reply: "The customer base is 5 million; if 10 percent of them buy, let's say with an aggressive marketing plan, etc., 500 thousand people buy the natural cosmetics cream at 40 euros because it is premium priced, you will have made 20 million euros in sales/top-line growth." The CEO would then have a rough estimate of whether this is a valuable endeavor or not. Usually, the situation that as a junior consultant you get to sit with the CEO and brainstorm about new products does not happen very often, but this method helps calculate the revenue/sales potential of any business undertaken.

Back to the story—The Estimation Case

I was back in the preparation room, and I was able to have a small break. I did not have one estimation case; I had two. For my first one, I was called into a tiny room, this time only with one interviewer. The room was not a conference room, it was more like an "I need a quiet space for a phone call" room. I remember the interviewer was sitting behind a table to the left when I walked in. So I turned and sat on the designated chair on the other side of the table. "Ok, here we go!" I remember thinking to myself, "I can do this." I always have to motivate myself. The cheerleaders we have in our lives cannot always be there for us, so we have to cheer for ourselves.

I said hello, and the lady said: "We only have 10 minutes; let's get started." She was also trying to put pressure on me, which worked like a charm. But I could do this, I had practiced, and then I went for it. I was asked to estimate how many electric sockets Germany has (see the example above). I had prepared how to solve estimation questions like these and would know how to answer for sure. I answered the estimation question, and in between, the interviewer reminded me how many minutes I had left. It was mean of her to hassle me like that. But then again, I have heard the stress tests are normal. I finished and the interviewer was happy with my final number and proceeded to tell me the correct answer. But I did not hear her anymore. I was already ready to leave. I just nodded. "Finally, one more piece to go," I thought. I went back to the preparation room while someone else was called in, and I sat and waited for the last part of my interview.

Then, I was called into the next room, where I was asked to prepare a cost calculation for 20 minutes. This interviewer was also a woman, but this time, she did not hassle me. "What a relief," I thought to myself. As I sat down, I said to myself: "I can do this, I can do this." I had to calculate the differences between buying and leasing a gas station.

I was given some financial information, but I had to think about what factors were relevant, and I had to assume the rest of the unknown variables. I was given 15 minutes alone, and I did not have a calculator, nor did I have my phone with me. But I practiced a lot before the interview, so I relied on my brain. I am not one of those people who are born with a mental arithmetic skill, but with practice, everything is possible. I managed to calculate everything on the whiteboard when the interviewer came back in. I rushed through my presentation because I only had five minutes to present. In the end, the interviewer asked me if I would rather rent the gas station, or if I would buy it. I really did not know at that moment, so I just guessed. The time was up anyway, but I think she just wanted me to commit to an answer. She nodded and said: "All good!" And I left the room.

"WHAT A DAY!" I just thought to myself as I walked to the kitchen to get a glass of water.

#girlconsultant lifehacks: For the Estimation Case

Do:

- Be your own cheerleader. Pep talk to yourself, go to the toilet, and do some power posing.
- Practice your math skills—long division, long multiplication, and fractions—ahead of time.

- If you have questions, ask. Avoid a blackout panic.
- Make assumptions confidently.

Don't:
- Let the interviewer stress you. They do it on purpose to see how nervous they can make you.
- Don't panic with time constraints; do as much as you can and wing the rest.
- Don't forget that you can calculate everything on paper.

Practice makes perfect—the estimation case

Once you understand the logic behind this part of the interview, I am sure you will master it. Here, it is important to practice dividing big numbers by percentages. When you divide, choose percentages that are easy to calculate. Try to avoid the 7.5 percent, the 13.8 percent, and so on. Round the numbers as much as you can. Say things like: "For the sake of the estimation, I am rounding up/down to xyz." If you are unsure about an assumption—for example, the population of Spain—ask the interviewer to give you a starting point. The more you practice, the better you will get at it. Since there is no real right answer in the end, work on the calculations and the structure of narrowing down a population number to a target group.

Pro Tips and Resources

- Find more practice estimation cases online.
- Go to YouTube and search "how to solve an estimation/market sizing case."

The brain teaser

A brain teaser is a type of interview question designed to challenge the candidate's critical thinking, creativity, and problem-solving abilities. Brain teasers are typically puzzles, riddles, or paradoxes that require the candidate to think outside the box and come up with a creative solution.

If you don't know, now you know:

A brain teaser is a type of interview question designed to challenge the candidate's critical thinking, creativity, and problem-solving abilities. Brain teasers are typically puzzles, riddles, or paradoxes that require the candidate to think outside the box and come up with a creative solution.

Interviewers may ask brain teasers to assess a candidate's ability to handle complex or unexpected problems, their level of persistence and determination when faced with a difficult challenge, and their ability to think creatively and come up with innovative solutions. Brain teasers can also reveal how a candidate approaches problems, how they break down problems into smaller components, and how they communicate their thought process.

However, it is important to note that brain teasers have been criticized for being unreliable and not necessarily predictive of job performance. Some argue that these types of questions may create unnecessary stress for candidates and not accurately reflect the skills needed for the role. Therefore, many companies have moved away from using brain teasers in interviews and instead focus on more job-specific questions and scenarios. As mentioned in the introduction of this chapter, before you go to the interview, call or write HR and ask what things you will be doing on the day of the interview.

To crack a brain teaser on the spot, you should be good at logical thinking and approach the question in a structured way, even if it might seem confusing and complex at the beginning. However, you can also practice/memorize the most popular brain teasers out there. Unless you are naturally just really good at this, practice these questions by going online and looking for "most common brain teasers for consulting interviews."

Test yourself: See if you can crack the brainteaser

Here is one example of a brain teaser: You had 10 pounds or 10 grams of cucumbers, each consisting of 99 percent water. After leaving them in the sun, some of the water in the cucumbers evaporated. If the cucumbers ended up with 98 percent water in them, how much of their weight did they lose?

Answer: The cucumbers lost half their weight. If the water is 99 percent of the total original weight, the remaining substance weighs 0.1 pounds/0.1 gram (1/100 of the total weight). If, after the evaporation, the remaining substance comprises 2 percent (1/50 of the cucumber), the total weight must be 50 * 0.1 pounds/gram = 5 pounds.

You probably wanted to solve the question with an easy rule of thirds, but that is the crux of these brainteasers, because mostly they are not what they seem to be.

For the most popular brain teasers, I will send you to any search engine. There are so many people who are so much better at explaining and walking you through these exercises than me.

#girlconsultant lifehacks: For the brainteaser

Do:

- Ask the interviewer if brainteasers will be part of the interview.
- If yes, look online and find more examples that you can practice or memorize.

- Practice long division and multiplication, as you probably will not have a calculator.

Don't:
- Panic, as everything can be learned, even if it is just for one interview.
- Don't believe that you will ever use this knowledge again).

Practice makes perfect—Brainteasers, like anything else, are a matter of practice. This seems like a lot to do for an interview, but I am sure it is worth it. Unless you are one of those people like a girl I remember in high school, who did brainteasers for fun in her spare time and are naturally really good at it, I think a weekend session to just watch, learn, and apply is in order.

tl;dr

- Consulting interviews are more focused on assessing your problem-solving capabilities and analytical skills with the help of different structures. They are about logically guiding your interviewer through your thought process.

- The personal motivation portion is the same everywhere. You talk about yourself, your career, your passions in life, and why you want to work in that specific field.

- The case study is when you are asked how you would solve a client's problem.

- The estimation case is a guestimate of a final number by starting with a known number, then making assumptions, rounding up or down as needed.

- Brainteasers are mathematical riddles that do not necessarily reflect job performance.

CHAPTER 7

What You Need to Know
After You Sign and
Before You Start

N
ow, girlfriend, let's talk about the things you should
know at signing time and before you step foot in the
office for your first day. In this chapter, I will give you
an overview of the most common contracts, how to get the
most money, what the organizational hierarchy looks like generally, how body leasing works, and what project work looks
like. This chapter material will help you get the best out of
your consulting contract and get oriented to your new career
in consulting much faster.

What this chapter will not cover is what the average day
or week looks like in a consulting career, because honestly,
there is no average. Each company and each project will run
differently in terms of what meetings you have, what hours
you work, whether you are required to be on-site or allowed
to work remotely, and any number of other variations. If you
want to know what a usual day or week will look like in your
consulting job, this is a perfect question to ask during the
interview or in the days before you begin. With that said . . .
let's start with MONEY.

Generally speaking, people talk very little about money—especially women. When it comes to jobs, the gender pay gap is real. In the U.S. in 2021, women as a whole earned 84 percent of what men earned, and do not get me started on how much lower that percentage was for women of color; this could take a while.[19] This is why I am including the details about general consulting contracts, the bonus, and the signing bonus (yes, you need to ask for it). I want to ensure you make the money you should. Plus, depending on your education, you should ask for the right position that will meet you where you are and learn from my friend, who failed to do so.

I am no lawyer, and contracts may vary depending on the country you live in, but I will tell you what the general concepts are. (Please do seek legal counsel for more details and specifics and to review your contracts.) To help you talk the talk and walk the walk, I have included general concepts of how the business of consulting works so that you can sound like you have been working in the industry for some time (which will also help you in negotiating the terms of your contract). People will be more inclined to negotiate if they can tell you know your stuff.

Let's go!

Contracts and accepting the position

It is very common for consulting companies to offer candidates a preliminary contract that states you have the intention

---

[19] Carolina Aragão, "Gender pay gap in US hasn't changed much in two decades," Pew Research Center, March 1, 2023, https://www.pewresearch.org/short-reads/2023/03/01/gender-pay-gap-facts/.

of signing with the company at the end of the interview. It is sort of a way to lock in their top talent because there is a lot of competition and companies want to make sure that you are committed. This does not mean you cannot go to the next company or the next interview and then also sign there because in the end, you are free to choose, but it is nice to have some sort of commitment from both sides.

It is common to apply for a position, such as a consultant for company XYZ, that is not department-specific or does not have a level attached to it. The company uses the interview to decide which department and at what level they think you belong. Attempt to gain an upfront knowledge of where you want to go, so you can push for that during the interview. To prepare, look at the company online to see if you can gauge the departments they have and generally what they do.

If you don't know, now you know:
Three things you need to watch out for
before you sign:

1. Make sure you agree with the department you are hired into: Management Consulting, Technical Consulting, Strategy, Project Management Office, Business Process Outsourcing, etc. These terms might mean different things

in different companies, so check online or by asking during the interviews what the different departments are.

2. Make sure you agree with the level that they are proposing to start you at. This means that if you already have working experience, challenge them on why the contract might be for an analyst or junior consultant. Also ask what the role description and responsibility is of the level above you.

3. Make sure you agree with the bonus structure, even if it is late in the day, and you just want to go home. Ask questions about what the bonus means. You can always renegotiate later; however, let them explain the details to you.

How I Accepted My Contract

After my last interview, I deflated like a balloon. I was so happy to be done! As I moved to the kitchen to drink some water, all the participants were asked to stand in a circle in the corridor between the kitchen and the offices. An HR representative announced: "We will now deliberate on who will get a preliminary offer. Please wait until your name is called. When it is called, join us in the room. Do not leave before." And so, we waited. Everyone was called in. Some made it; others did not. I was the last one to get called into the room.

They handed me a preliminary contract which I was thrilled to sign then and there. Signing immediately was security for me, because what if they woke up the next day and changed their mind about hiring me? That said, I did not *really* read through the contract; my brain was mush from the whole day. Let's say I *skimmed* through it. I was sure that there were always ways to get out of the contract if I needed to, and the reality was that I did not have any other offers in the pipeline, so I could not pick and choose anyway.

So, I signed, and I made sure I signed with the supply chain department. I had studied supply chain, and it was something I wanted to work in. I was very specific about it when they asked me, whereas my future colleague was not. She was unaware of the different departments, and she did not specify. What a shame, because they stuck her in PMO, the Project Management Office. The PMO was basically a department relegated to taking care of everyone and everything around the project. In other words, doing everything except working on the project. An example would be to organize the branded team cups—yes, actual cups for drinking—to make sure everyone had accommodations for travel, buy flowers for clients on their birthdays, etc.

My friend who did not specify a department preference also got paid less than me, because she did not sign herself into the Management Consulting department, or better, the Strategy department. It was just a technicality at the beginning because her priority was getting in, no matter what, even though she had amazing qualifications. It made her life miserable, because having studied marketing and being very smart, she was bored after two months. She tried everything to change roles internally and tried to offer her time and brain power after hours to support the team on the marketing content side of things, but they took advantage of her goodwill and nothing changed for her. Eventually, she got burned out. This should be a learning experience for all of us. We have to get informed about what we want to do, and then we have to say what we want!

The overtime contract

From my experience, there are two types of contracts: one with overtime, and one without. Sometimes you can choose a type, sometimes you cannot. Be sure to check on your local labor laws. If you can choose a type, then think about what is more important to you, time or money. The contract with overtime basically means you have your 40-hour work week at an equivalent pay. Any hour you work beyond that you can record as overtime and either choose to be paid for it or choose to take an equal amount of time off. This is a great option if you are planning on taking two to three months' paid leave to go traveling at some point. Depending on the company, you will take a year or two to accumulate so many overtime hours. Between projects, it is easy to just take a long vacation, because usually you will be waiting for your next project to be sold, and then you can get staffed on. This option is clearly for the people who value time more than money. Think about the fact that you will probably accumulate airline miles and hotel miles; it would be a shame if you could not make use of the travel statuses on your own time.

If you get offered one type but prefer the other, then you should ask if switching is a possibility.

My Overtime Contract

My contract was an overtime one, and my pay was a good beginner's salary by German standards. In the beginning, I just signed whatever was laid in front of me, because I did not know about the signing bonus (more later), and I did not know the pros and cons of overtime versus no overtime.

135

While working, we had to record our hours in a system every 15 days and say what project we worked on, so that the hours could be deducted from the project budget. I usually worked (and then consequently recorded) one or two overtime hours every day.

In the end, I had accumulated so many hours, I could take three months off. I used those three months to work on my very first Kickstarter Campaign for my own company, Corner Office (more in chapter 14). I could have equally gone backpacking through Thailand, but back then, my dedication to hustling was real. Still, all those hours were totally put to use in a way I felt good about.

The contract without overtime

The contract without overtime is the one where you get a higher base salary, as your overtime hours are already included in your compensation. With this version, it is expected that you do overtime, but since no one records it, you might also be on a more relaxed project and not do any. The only catch is that you will only have the standard amount of vacation days available, so you will not be able to take, for example, three months off. You can always take a sabbatical, but depending on the company policy, this may only be possible at a specific level. This option is for the people who want to make some money, so think about it.

Choosing this contract is your call, if it is something you can negotiate. Pick whatever is more important to you, time versus money. If there is no option to pick a specific type of contract, ask for the one you want; maybe there is a way to get it. Do not be afraid to ask. They have invested a lot of money in recruiting, and they have handed you an offer. They want to hire you; you cannot lose the job offer now.

#girlconsultant lifehack:

If you have the option to choose, decide whether you prefer a contract with or without overtime. If you're not given the option, ask for it. Do not be afraid to ask; they have invested a lot of money in recruiting, and they have handed you an offer.

Signing bonus and the general bonus

The main difference between a signing bonus and a general bonus is the timing of the payment and the purpose of the bonus.

A *signing bonus* is a one-time payment that is typically made when a new employee joins a company and is designed to attract top talent to the organization. The signing bonus is often used to offset any costs associated with joining the company, such as relocation expenses or a gap in employment. The amount of a signing bonus is typically negotiated as part of the initial job offer and is usually paid out in a lump sum after the employee has started working for the company.

If you don't know, now you know:

A *signing bonus* is a one-time payment that is typically made when a new employee joins a company and is designed to attract top talent to the organization.

Companies generally do not offer you signing bonuses right off the bat. You should ask for one, either directly asking: "Will I receive a signing bonus?" or simply telling a compelling story, that may or may not be totally true: "I have an offer from another consulting company, and I would be turning down more money. I would like to come and work for you though, because you have a better culture. Would you be open to giving me a signing bonus?"

The amount usually depends on the country and company. For beginners, it is around 5 to 10 percent of the annual salary. Depending on when and where you are reading this book, a quick internet search to confirm this could be in order.

A *general bonus* is typically paid out to employees who have already been with the company for a certain period of time, usually as a reward for their performance or as an incentive to stay with the company. General bonuses may be paid out annually, quarterly, or on some other schedule and are typically based on the employee's individual performance, the company's overall performance, or a combination of the two.

If you don't know, now you know:

A *general bonus* is typically paid out to employees who have already been with the company for a certain period of time, usually as a reward for their performance or as an incentive to stay with the company.

The amount of the general bonus really depends on the company you are working for. I can only say that from my experience, my bonuses were very little throughout the years. From what I had heard, if you are a big consulting company, on a global level, the bonuses are distributed amongst the countries, and then the managing directors take their share, then the senior manager/junior partners, and so on. Thus, by the time it reaches you, down at the bottom, there is not that much left. You get the gist. Now I could be wrong, depending on where you are while reading this, but take note to ask this before signing. Usually, they will tell you that the bonus on average is X high, and this will come on top of your salary. Make sure you ask the question, "Under what circumstances would I not receive the annual bonus?"

Both signing bonuses and general bonuses are designed to incentivize employees. Make sure that, alongside your salary, you have asked for a signing bonus and that you are clear on how and when the annual bonus is paid out.

Organizational hierarchies

Before moving on to the staffing process, let's take a quick look at the hierarchies, so you know what I am talking about when I speak of a manager. In consulting, being a manager is a big deal; it takes time and effort to become one, and tied to it is a specific skill set. Unlike businesses outside of consulting, one cannot simply become a manager straight out of college or university. Usually, you start as an analyst, though it is possible for PhDs to start as consultants. In consulting, there are typically several levels of the organization's hierarchy, which vary somewhat depending on the firm and the country. Here are the most common levels you might find in a consulting firm:

Partners
Senior Managers
Managers
Consultants
Analysts

Analyst/Junior Consultant

This is the entry-level position in consulting, typically for recent college graduates or those with one year of work experience. Analysts often work on project teams and assist more senior consultants in research, analysis, and presentations.

Consultant

Consultants are generally the next level up from analysts. They typically have two to four years of experience and take on more responsibility in managing projects and client relationships.

Senior Consultant/Junior Manager

Senior consultants typically have four to six years of experience and take on a leadership role in project management and client relationships. They may also have responsibility for supervising and coaching junior team members.

Manager/Project Manager

Managers have five to seven years of experience and are responsible for managing multiple projects and teams, as well as developing and maintaining client relationships. They also often play a role in business development, such as identifying new clients or opportunities for growth.

Senior Manager/Junior Partner

This is a more senior leadership position in consulting, with eight to twelve or more years of experience. Senior managers and directors are responsible for leading large consulting engagements, managing client relationships at the executive level, and overseeing the work of multiple teams.

Partner/Managing Director

Partners or principals are the most senior leaders in a consulting firm. They are often responsible for the overall strategy and direction of the firm, as well as managing key client relationships and developing new business opportunities. In smaller companies, they have also bought into the company, and therefore own a part of the company.

It is worth noting that the titles and levels may differ slightly from one consulting firm to another, but these are some of the most common levels you may encounter in the industry.

Before you negotiate your contract, check how the hierarchy is structured in the company that you are applying to. Go on LinkedIn and follow some people working there. What are their titles and how much work experience do they have? Also, do not be afraid to ask them for insights into the company, even if their title might sound fancy. These people still put their pants on one leg at a time.

If you don't know, now you know:

Before you negotiate your contract, check how the hierarchy levels are in the company that you are applying to. Go on LinkedIn and follow some people working there. What are their titles and how much work experience do they have? Also, do not be afraid to ask them for insights into the company, even if their title might sound fancy.

Body leasing: how to get staffed

Before I get into the details, I need to tell you how "body leasing" works in consulting.

Often, working in consulting is compared to being a sex worker. Hear me out on this one. You have clients who tell you what they want you to do (i.e., they hire you to solve a specific issue they have); you have bosses (a.k.a. the pimps) who collect the money the client pays for your services; and you are sent (pimped out) to work for a client, based on the set of skills you bring to the table. Do you see what I'm getting at?

In consulting, you sell a service, and the service is your brainpower. That brainpower, unlike any other service, cannot really be quantified, because people cannot see INTO your brain. It is not an electrician who comes to your house and fixes the lamps, or someone who drills the holes into your wall to hang the paintings. The qualification that you gained at school and uni, your curiosity and willingness to learn, and the speed at which you grasp new things—all this is why a consulting company hires you and then farms you out to clients to help them solve their business problems. Do not worry—you have all these things; otherwise, you would not have gotten the job offer.

You make money if you are chargeable/billable

First off, the terms "chargeable" and "billable" can be used interchangeably—it depends on what consulting company you work for and the word they use. When you are on a project, the consulting company leases/rents/pimps you out to the customer, and then the client pays an hourly or daily rate for you to your employer. This means you are chargeable/billable because your salary is paid from the money that the client is paying for your work on the project. What is not paid out as your salary or project-related expenses is then pocketed by your employer and declared as profit.

If you don't know, now you know:

You are chargeable/billable because your salary is paid from the money that the client is paying for your work on the project.

Thus, the intention of the company is to always have you on a project for them to make money. Usually, you have to book your time somewhere. Every 15 days, you have to hand in your so-called "timesheet," where you record your time on different projects.

How to get onto a project

In general, projects are sold by managing directors or senior managers, sometimes even by managers, but this depends on the company setup. I have heard that in the MBB consulting companies, only managing directors sell projects, whereas at the Big Four, consultants have to sell to get promoted to manager.

This is why, as mentioned in chapter 2, consulting is a great choice, because you can have fate decide on what projects you will be staffed on. In some companies, someone will just call you out of the blue for a project that does not align with your expertise, just because the manager is desperate and needs a resource. In other companies, however, you are part of someone's industry practice and the head of the practice will not lend you to other practices, because you are on her payroll.

Staffing: What to Expect When You Get the "Project Call"

Getting staffed onto a project usually works the same way each time. The project leader goes through the staffing list and upon seeing that you are available and what your field of study/interest is (you have uploaded your CV into the company's internal database and added your field of interests, certifications, etc.), she will call you. The "call" usually goes like this . . . as you read, pay attention to the things in italics. These are things you will say or information you will receive about the project on one of these calls.

I was sitting in the office in Düsseldorf, Germany, and I was just about to get a coffee. I left my phone at my desk, but just as I walked through the door of the kitchen, I could hear it ring.

I answer.

"Hello?"

"Hi, this is Kyoko calling; am I speaking to Tanja? I am a senior manager for: *(insert industry group here)*."

"Yes, this is she," I replied.

"I am calling to let you know that I have a project for you."

"Great! Tell me about the project," I replied eagerly.

"Well, it is a project at a company called *(insert company name here)* located in *(insert town here)* and you are requested to be on-site *(insert how many days of travel a week)*. The scope of the project is: *(insert scope of project)* and your role would be: *(insert role and scope of work)*," Kyoko said.

She went into all the details because she already had a position for me in mind. However, I could still negotiate.

"Thank you so much for the elaboration, Kyoko, and thank you for considering me. How did you find me? And based on what skills do you think I would be a good fit?" I asked, because in the end, it is not THAT simple to get me for any task. *Snaps fingers*

"Well, Tanja, I need someone for: *(insert scope of work)* and in our staffing list, you were mentioned to have experience in this field. Could you elaborate on your experience?"

"Of course, I can elaborate *(insert a story of this experience or insert story of how you want to learn that skill, and what makes you the right person to bring onto the project. Or, if you do not want the project: Insert story how this is not your thing).*"

"Great! I am happy you are on board. We start the project on Monday, please be at this address *(insert client address)* at 9 a.m."

"Please send me the Statement of Work and the project outline, if you have it, so I can prepare for Monday," I said, because I like to know what is going on.

"Yes, of course! See you Monday!"

We hung up.

Well, that was it. I was staffed on a project. I had to organize my flights, my hotel, and what to wear on my first week.

First things first, though. As soon as I got the Statement of Work, I read it, so that I knew what the project was about. Everything else that I needed to know, they told me the following Monday.

tl;dr

- Clearly state your preferred department during the interview to align with your interests, and check the preliminary offer to ensure you are in the department you requested.
- Choose between contracts with or without overtime based on your preferences (assuming you have the right to choose).
- Always request a signing bonus.
- Inquire about the bonus structure so you understand the company's bonus system from the beginning.
- Familiarize yourself with the company's hierarchical levels and your place among the ranks.
- Seek projects that align with your interests and skills.
- Go kick some butt!

Bonus: Consulting lingo (a.k.a. Bullshit Bingo)

For something fun to wrap up this second part, I will help you talk the talk. Every company and profession has its own lingo, jargon, and abbreviations. Once you are on the project, you will notice every client you work for will have different words they overuse. At the beginning, it seems a little confusing, but let me get you started with the consulting lingo.

Consulting lingo refers to the specialized language and jargon used by consultants in their work. This language is often filled with buzzwords, acronyms, and technical terms specific to the consulting industry, which means it is usually difficult for someone outside of consulting to know what they're talking about.

Consulting lingo can be used to communicate complex ideas and strategies quickly and efficiently among team members and clients. It can also serve as a way for consultants to demonstrate their expertise and differentiate themselves from others in the field. Examples of common consulting terms and phrases include "scope creep," "deliverable," "value proposition," "synergy," "best practices," "strategic alignment," "thought leadership," and "client engagement." I have provided a full list at the end of the chapter.

There is an art for how to use these words in a sentence, because when used correctly, the sentences can become very powerful. When these words are overused, the sentence just becomes plain vanilla and doesn't mean anything. Many people just use the words as fillers in sentences.

Here is one example where you can see the consultant used several industry-terms that made it difficult for the client to understand:

During a meeting with a client, a consultant was discussing the project timeline and stated, "We need to circle back with the stakeholders and get their buy-in on the next phase. Once we have achieved that, we can move forward with the deliverables and keep the project on track." The client responded with a puzzled look and asked the consultant to clarify what they meant by "stakeholders," "circle back," "buy-in," and "deliverables."

In comparison, the consultant could have said:

"We need to talk with the other people on this project and make sure they are okay with the next phase of the project. Once we have their agreement, we can move forward with the specific tasks and keep the project on schedule."

You can see the difference, of course. Once you are in consulting, it can be easy to slip into industry-speak and forget your audience, or be very conscious of when colleagues are over-using it. It is quite fun, though, to know how to speak the language; it is like speaking a secret code that no outsiders can understand.

Introducing Bullshit Bingo

Most of us know the game of Bingo, where a caller pulls random numbers, and you try to match those to numbers on your card to get a sequence of five numbers in a row (horizontal, vertical, or diagonal). The first person to do so yells BINGO! and wins a prize. In consulting, we have Bullshit Bingo. It is an insider's game that people sometimes play quietly but everyone knows about. Sometimes, people play during meetings, presentations, or speeches, marking off buzzwords or jargon (words commonly used in a particular industry or context) on a premade bingo card. The goal of the game is to mark off a full row or column of buzzwords to complete the bingo and "win" the game. See below for a full bingo card.

When the game is played in secret, it is a way to inject humor into a meeting or presentation and to poke fun at the overuse of buzzwords or jargon. However, it can also serve as a way to highlight the need for clearer communication and to encourage presenters to use language that is accessible to everyone.

I sometimes played Bullshit Bingo in a three-and-a-half-hour alignment meeting we used to have on Thursday afternoons in the summer. It was the jour-fixe of the week, and all the project streams were invited to join—about ten of us in total. Everyone had their turn to present their weekly to-dos. This was my first project, and I did not really have much to say, because my manager presented the items we accomplished during the week. In this meeting, we were tracked against the project plan that had been set up to accomplish the project. Every team took their turn, and my colleague and I noticed that the project manager kept overusing the words/phrases "low-hanging fruit," "stakeholder alignment," "deliverables," and "circle back."

After one hour, the project manager had already used at least five of each of those words. I was already looking outside the window, ready to go home. We were on the fourth floor, I was in a suit, and it was boiling hot in there. Plus, it was the afternoon. So, between being super-hot and getting toward the end of the day, I was also bored. Hardly able to keep my eyes open because of the long nights they made us work from Monday to Wednesday, my colleague sent me a link via the internal chat to play bullshit bingo together online. I logged on, and in a matter of minutes, my face lit up and I mouthed "Bingo" to my colleague, who was sitting next to me, so we started giggling, but we tried not to be too loud so no one would notice. The meeting went on forever that day, and we played more rounds of bingo. It was a good day.

To not deprive you of such a unique and fun bonding experience between you and your colleagues, here is a list of consulting lingo words explained. If you want to go one step further, look later in this chapter for the bullshit bingo card.

Bullshit Bingo legend

In any meeting, these words will come up a dozen times, and although you know what they mean, the sheer number of times they are said is comical. So, whenever you are bored in a meeting, play bullshit bingo. You are welcome.

A:

A-B Testing: Also known as split testing, it is a method of comparing two versions of a web page or app against each other to determine which one performs better and yields higher results.

Actionable insights: Information or data-driven findings that can be directly applied to improve a situation or decision-making process.

Agile: This term originated in programming, together with the agile methodologies. Agile can be used in terms of scrum or agile project management, where a project is organized in weekly or two-week sprints.

B:

Billable/chargeable: It refers to the hours or services that a consultant can invoice to a client for their work on a specific project or task. These are the hours that directly contribute to revenue generation for the consulting firm. Non-billable hours, on the other hand, typically include administrative tasks, training, or internal meetings that do not directly generate income but are essential for the operation of the consulting firm.

Big data: Large and complex data sets that require specialized processing tools to extract meaningful insights.

Big picture: It means to zoom out on an issue or topic and look at it from a strategic or bird's-eye perspective. It means abstracting the issue to a point where you can put it into perspective to see/deduct what comes before and after the topic and to analyze what impact it may have on other areas.

Blocking points: Blocking points in consulting refer to obstacles, challenges, or issues that hinder the progress of a consulting project or prevent it from moving forward smoothly.

C:

Change management: The structured approach to transitioning individuals, teams, and organizations from the current state to a desired future state.

Circle of influence: It represents the group of stakeholders whom a person or organization can directly affect or have an impact on through their actions or decisions. These stakeholders are within the sphere of control or influence of the individual or entity creating the stakeholder map. Understanding the circle of influence helps prioritize efforts and resources for effective stakeholder management by focusing on those who can be directly engaged or whose opinions and actions can be influenced.

Core competency: The primary area of expertise or capability that sets a company apart from competitors.

D:

Deep dive: Also called root-cause analysis; a classic way is to ask "why" five times. This generally means to look at the numbers, see where they are coming from, and explain to yourself why they are this high/low, or how they compare to the average.

Deliverables: Tangible results or outputs that a project or task is expected to produce.

E:

Elevator pitch: A concise and compelling summary used to introduce a product, service, or idea in a short time span, such as an elevator ride.

End-to-end: When thinking of a process, you always have a beginning and an end. This keyword refers to being able to see how the issue you are currently working on is influenced by or impacts the previous and later stages of the process.

EOD/EOB: End of day, or end of business. This is a term used frequently to describe a deadline for a task. Since in consulting, the end of business is usually the end of the day, these terms are used interchangeably. In a nine-to-five job, you would call five o'clock the end of business.

Escalation: When something is blocking the progress of the project, you need to tell your manager or client counterpart about it (escalate the situation up), so that she can solve the situation.

F:

Fast track: This is a term for people who get promoted quickly. Can also be used as: for projects that are approved/staffed/worked quickly, possibly skipping some usual approval processes (e.g., a senior leader's pet project).

G:

Game changer: A disruptive idea, strategy, or innovation that fundamentally alters the dynamics of an industry or market.

Governance: Describes the organizational structure in terms of who reports to whom. When doing a reorganization, this is a necessary step to define the roles and their circle of influence.

H:

Hot desk: You do not have an assigned desk in the office; every time you come in, you sit somewhere else. It's hot because you only sit on it for a day.

J:

Jour-fixe: The weekly meeting you have with the client to go through the tasks you did last week, the ones you will do next week, and any risks or blocking points.

L:

Lean: A term coming from Lean Six Sigma, a methodology on how to run operations in a company as efficiently and perfectly as possible, without a lot of unnecessary steps.

Leverage: To use something to the maximum advantage, such as resources, technology, or innovation.

Low-hanging fruit/quick wins: Terms used to describe the usual monetary gain you can bring the client if you change some small things quickly. Also, ways to gain quick progress or things that will bring bonus goodwill (for instance, with customers or local governments) with little or no effort.

M:

Mission critical: Refers to tasks, activities, or systems that are essential and crucial for the successful operation and fulfillment of an organization's mission or objectives.

Moving the needle: Creating a noticeable and substantial impact on a particular outcome or performance indicator.

O:

Outside the box: Thinking creatively and unconventionally to find innovative solutions or ideas.

P:

PlsFix: When your manager sends you an email with an attached PowerPoint slide and asks you to "fix" them. This means she wants you to make them visually appealing, check for typos, align boxes, make sure the header and footer are in the right place, etc.

Proactive: Taking initiative and anticipating future needs or challenges, rather than merely reacting to events as they occur.

R:

ROI: Return on investment is a financial term. When calculating a business case, the ROI needs to be clear for the client to show the benefit of the project—how much more money/customer satisfaction/employee retention benefits the client because of your project.

S:

Scrum way of working: Scrum is an agile project management framework that focuses on delivering value through iterative development. It divides work into time-boxed units called sprints, usually lasting two to four weeks, during which a cross-functional team collaborates to build a product incrementally. Scrum emphasizes regular inspection and adaptation, with a focus on transparency, communication, and flexibility to meet changing requirements.

(Agile) Sprint: At the beginning of each sprint the list of customer requirements is created according to priorities, and during the sprint, the tasks are then completed. At the end of a sprint, the outcome is reviewed by the client. This is an iterative way to build software or manage a project.

Steering committee: A group of stakeholders or senior executives responsible for providing guidance, direction, and decision-making on important projects or strategic initiatives.

Synergy: Similar to win-win, is used frequently to describe a business situation or rationalize any decision. One of those fluff words that basically means that you try to leverage each other's strengths to come to the best possible outcome.

T:

Thought leadership: Establishing oneself or a company as a recognized authority and innovative thinker in a specific field.

Timesheet: As a consultant you earn money for the company if you are billable/chargeable. This means that you are on a project and the client is paying your daily fee. It needs to be transparent how much you work, and you need to book your hours on specific projects. You hand in your timesheet, usually in the middle of and the end of the month. If you forget, you get a million emails reminding you.

V:

Value add: An additional benefit or enhancement that increases the worth or quality of a product, service, or project.

W:

Win-win: This term is used to describe a situation where the parties involved are each pursuing their own interest but are meeting somewhere in the middle with a specific decision so that both parties get something out of it.

Numbers:

360-degree view: A comprehensive and all-encompassing perspective that considers multiple angles or viewpoints.

5 whys: A problem-solving technique involving repetitive questioning to identify the root cause.

#girlconsultant lifehacks: Bullshit Bingo Card Template

360-degree view	A-B testing	Timesheet	Deep dive	Fast track
5 whys	Low-hanging fruit	Win-win	Big data	Thought leadership
Synergy	Leverage	ROI	Circle of influence	Lean
Scrum	PlsFix	Proactive	Governance	Mission critical
Agile	EOD	Escalation	Jour-fixe	Steering committee

PART 3:

SETTING YOURSELF UP
FOR SUCCESS

CHAPTER 8

Empowering Yourself
Through Assertiveness

Are you familiar with the term *assertiveness*? I had never heard of it until I was well into my 20s. My best friend Bianca, an associate professor and head of psychology at a university in London, told me about it. What Bianca shared with me instantly piqued my interest, and I knew this was something worth delving into.

We were on a summer girls' trip (one of the guaranteed annual highlights in our calendars), and as always, we had one of those fun, bossed-up but intellectual conversations. I was telling her about my newfound obsession with power suits and how wearing them to the office helped me feel and act more confidently, but then again, sometimes a suit alone didn't cut it. Bianca told me about what it meant to be assertive. Drawing from her experience providing assertiveness training for businesses, which taught employees how to navigate complex clients and challenging situations, she outlined how being assertive can be used to enhance communication and ultimately lead to more self-confidence.

This knowledge on assertiveness was so insightful that, with a lot of trial and error and constant improvement, it has helped me become a better version of myself ever since. I became more confident in expressing myself clearly, minimizing room for misinterpretation; I found the strength to assertively decline requests (saying "no" more often); and I grew more confident at work. Naturally, I had to share this with you, from one girl-friend to another.

As you've figured out by now, this chapter focuses on asser-tiveness—what it is, different levels of assertiveness, different types of bosses, how confidence and assertiveness pair well together, and ultimately, why being assertive is ridiculously helpful as a woman in consulting. This chapter is where it's at. If you want to learn ONE main thing that can help you in your consulting career, learn how to be assertive!

So what exactly is being assertive?

Imagine this: Alex, a talented consultant, often hesitated to communicate her ideas and wasn't very clear in setting expec-tations with the client. When issues arose, Alex was reluctant to directly address them, fearing it might upset the client. As a result, the project faced frequent miscommunications and delays, causing frustration for both the client and the consulting team.

This scenario emphasizes the crucial role that assertiveness plays in the consulting world. But let's figure out first what assertiveness really is. Assertiveness is a vital social skill that relies on effective communication while respecting the thoughts and wishes of others. People who possess assertiveness commu-nicate their wants, needs, positions, and boundaries clearly and respectfully, leaving no doubt as to where they stand on any given topic. Assertive people experience fewer anxious thoughts, even in stressful situations, and respond to positive and negative emotions without becoming aggressive or resorting to passivity.

> ## If you don't know, now you know:
>
> Assertiveness is a vital social skill that relies on effective communication while respecting the thoughts and wishes of others. People who possess assertiveness communicate their wants, needs, positions, and boundaries clearly and respectfully.

Assertive individuals are not afraid to defend their points of view and goals or to influence others to see their side. They welcome both compliments and constructive criticism and can enhance their assertiveness through practical exercises and experience.

Being assertive means setting boundaries and communicating wishes without making demands or lashing out if requests are not met. This skill empowers you to approach others and stand up for yourself or others in a non-aggressive way; offering protection from bullies, for example. Clearly, assertiveness is a crucial element for success in personal and professional relationships. Makes sense, right?

A dynamite duo: assertiveness and confidence

Assertiveness and confidence are related but not the same thing. Assertiveness refers to the ability to express your thoughts, feelings, and opinions in a clear and direct manner while respecting the rights and opinions of others. Confidence, on the other hand, refers to a belief in oneself and one's abilities. It involves having a positive self-image and a sense of assurance in one's actions and decisions.

While assertiveness can be a result of confidence, it is possible to be assertive without feeling confident. Likewise, it is possible to be confident without being assertive. For example, someone may feel confident in their abilities but struggle to communicate their thoughts and opinions effectively. Similarly, someone may be able to speak up for themselves and set boundaries but still struggle with self-doubt and low self-esteem.

Of course, the goal is to be both assertive and confident. Maybe you feel that you are not that confident yet. Focus on being assertive and the confidence will come automatically—kind of like "fake it until you make it." Why does this phrase work?

By emulating assertive behavior in front of others, even when you might not initially feel that level of confidence internally, you can eventually grow into that role. Faking assertiveness is primarily about adopting the behaviors associated with assertiveness. This might mean you want to practice maintaining good eye contact, use a firm and clear tone of voice, and actively engage in conversations or negotiations at and outside of work that ensure you get what you want (but make sure both parties are happy with the resolution). When you behave in an assertive manner, you not only appear confident to others but also send a signal to your own mind that you are capable of handling the situation. Makes sense, right?

POP QUIZ! Which Type of Assertive Are You?

Before I explain the different levels of assertiveness to you, you should find out where you tend to fall on the assertiveness "scale." Fill out this questionnaire that Bianca and I designed to see what tendencies you have. Bear in mind that we exhibit different levels of assertiveness in different situations, so regardless of your result, it does not necessarily mean that you are ALWAYS like that. Also, keep in mind that you can work on becoming assertive regardless of your results at this moment.

1. When someone disagrees with you, how do you usually respond?

   a. Listen to their perspective and try to find common ground.

   b. Avoid confrontation and change the topic.

   c. Agree with them outwardly but feel resentful inside.

   d. Argue back and defend your point aggressively.

2. How do you handle criticism or feedback?

   a. Accept it gracefully and use it constructively.

   b. Appear unaffected but harbor resentment.

   c. Get defensive and feel hurt.

   d. Respond with anger or counter-criticism.

3. In a group decision-making situation, how likely are you to express your opinions?

   a. Always voice your thoughts and contribute actively.

   b. Stay quiet and let others decide.

   c. Agree with the majority but secretly disagree.

   d. Push your ideas forcefully, sometimes dominating the discussion.

4. How do you handle requests from others that you don't want to fulfill?

   a. Politely decline and offer an alternative solution.

   b. Give in to the request even if it inconveniences you.

   c. Agree reluctantly and feel burdened.

   d. Refuse bluntly and without consideration for their feelings.

5. How do you handle making mistakes or admitting when you are wrong?

   a. Acknowledge your mistakes and take responsibility.

   b. Feel ashamed and apologize excessively.

   c. Use humor or deflect blame onto others.

   d. Refuse to admit mistakes and blame others.

6. When negotiating, how do you advocate for your needs and interests?

   a. Clearly express your needs and preferences.

   b. Agree to what the other person wants to avoid conflict.

   c. Agree to the other person's terms but feel resentful.

   d. Insist on your demands without considering the other person's viewpoint.

7. How do you handle saying "no" to others?

   a. Comfortably and without guilt.

   b. Feel guilty and struggle to decline.

   c. Say "yes" but later find ways to avoid fulfilling the request.

   d. Say "no" bluntly and without regard for the other person's feelings.

8. How do you handle compliments or praise from others?

   a. Accept it graciously and thank the person.

   b. Downplay your achievements and feel unworthy.

   c. Brush off the compliment and make self-deprecating remarks.

   d. Reject the compliment and point out your flaws.

9. How do you handle personal boundaries being crossed by others?

   a. Firmly communicate your boundaries and ask others to respect them.

   b. Ignore the boundary violation and feel uncomfortable.

   c. Make indirect comments or withdraw affection.

   d. React angrily and confront the person aggressively.

10. How do you handle making decisions in a group setting?

    a. Offer your opinions and consider others' viewpoints.

b. Agree with the majority to avoid disagreement.

c. Say nothing but feel resentful if the decision does not go your way.

d. Insist on your ideas without considering others' opinions.

Scoring:

Count how many times you have circled a, b, c, and d answers. Write the answers in the circles below to see which type of assertiveness you gravitate toward. Usually, you are more than one type. Please do not judge yourself if you are not 100 percent assertive. Perfect assertiveness across all situations is very difficult to achieve. In different situations, depending on our moods, and/or our levels of stress, we may be one or the other. Take this exercise to self-reflect and to be honest with yourself. Ask: Who do I want to become? Then, by being aware, you can calibrate and work toward becoming the person you would like to be.

Different levels of assertiveness

Now that you know what your tendency is, I will give you a deep dive into the different levels of assertiveness and how to work with them. I have paired each level of assertiveness with an animal, because the explanation is just so fitting based on the respective animal's typical behaviors in nature: Passive (deer),

Assertive (dolphin), Passive-Aggressive (cat), and Aggressive (lion). This specific animal to level of assertiveness pairing is what Bianca uses in her lectures.[20]

Passive:

A passive level of assertiveness, according to Collins English Dictionary, is to not take action but instead let things happen. It means not acknowledging or expressing feelings, and it is letting other people violate your personal rights.[21]

---

[20] Maurice Lorr and William W. More, "Four dimensions of assertiveness," *Multivariate Behavioral Research* 15, no. 2 (1980): 127-138.
[21] "Definition of 'passive'", *Collins Dictionary*, 23.10.2024, https://www.collinsdictionary.com/dictionary/english/passive

How do they respond to criticism?	"I am so sorry—you are right, it is all my fault. I am so stupid!"
How do they engage with their environment and peers?	Sometimes, deers let themselves be walked all over, because they are SO nice. They want to be liked by everyone, so they do things for others, even though it would hurt them. They usually cannot show their feelings.
What do they think?	"You are OK; I am not OK."
What is their body language like?	They tend to avoid looking people in the eyes, speak in a soft voice, and sometimes stumble over their words. Their voice wobbles, and their body slumps, slouches, and fidgets.
How are they perceived by their peers?	They are seen as a pushover, spineless, passive, unassertive, shy, timid, afraid, or apologetic.

How to work with a passive person:

Working with passive people can be challenging, but there are several strategies you can use to effectively collaborate with them:

Encourage them to speak up: Passive people may be reluctant to share their opinions or ideas. Encourage them to participate in discussions and express their thoughts by asking open-ended questions and actively listening to their responses. When you are in a meeting and you notice the person has not said anything or not much, ask them what they think.

Provide clear expectations: Clearly define your expectations and the goals you want to achieve. This will help passive individuals understand what is expected of them and provide a framework for their contributions.

Break tasks into manageable steps: Passive individuals may feel overwhelmed by large tasks. Break down tasks into smaller, more manageable steps and clearly define their role in each step.

Offer support and resources: Provide passive individuals with the support and resources they need to complete tasks. This can include training, tools, or guidance from other team members.

Acknowledge their contributions: Recognize and appreciate the contributions of passive individuals. Celebrate their achievements and encourage them to continue to contribute to the team.

Create trust: Create trust by opening up first and showing vulnerability; the passive person can relate to you more, and communication will be easier and more efficient.

#girlconsultant lifehacks:

Working with a passive colleague: Remember that it is important to be patient and understanding when working with passive individuals. By providing support, encouragement, and clear expectations, you can help them become more engaged and active team members.

The Time I Had a Passive Phase at Work

As mentioned in the intro, we all go through ups and downs, and this book is not about all my successes, but also about the times I was on the struggle bus. I had a short phase in my life when I was passive. It all started at the end of my first project, when someone gave me feedback that I was too loud and had too much of an opinion. I took that feedback for my next project and became quiet; I became passive. I tried to avoid all confrontations and discussions; I thought my ideas were not valid, until someone on the new project said to me, "You never say anything, so what value-add do you have?" That intimidated me even more, so I said even less. I did not speak about my achievements; I did not speak about what topics I would like to work on . . . my assertive self had temporarily fallen into a deep, deep sleep, and the only way to snap out of it and to wake up was to switch projects. New client, new team, new boss. Back to my old "loud" self.

My lessons from this experience: Stay authentic. Not every feedback is good feedback (more on that in chapter 10) and the beauty of switching projects and clients is that it can help you snap out of a habit that has crept in without you knowing it. As I moved on to my third project and regained my confidence, I passed by the Hermès store and bought a lovely white and gold bangle. This bangle was to remind me to stay confident and assertive, even if someone tried to make me small to make themselves feel bigger.

Assertive:

Collins English Dictionary describes assertive people as stating their own needs and opinions clearly for other people to take notice.[22] They express their opinions in a calm, direct, and honest manner, without intentionally hurting someone else's feelings. It is kind of the "best way to be."

[22] "Definition of 'assertive'", *Collins Dictionary*, 23.10.2024, https://www.collins-dictionary.com/dictionary/english/assertive

How do they respond to criticism?	"Yes, you are right, I did this [was too fast/critical/ inconsiderate]. I feel it might be better if we did XYZ."
How do they engage with their environment and peers?	They state their needs and wants clearly, appropriately, and respectfully. They are able to stand up for themselves and say how they feel. They can say "no" without feeling guilty.
What do they think?	"You are okay; I am okay."
What is their body language like?	Comfortable with direct eye contact, they are relaxed, with an upright posture and straight shoulders. They smile when appropriate, with a firm but warm voice. They nod and acknowledge people's facial reactions.
How are they perceived by their peers?	They feel in control of themselves and their own life but are connected to others; they are perceived as confident, honest, and mature and are typically liked by others.

How to work with an assertive person:

Working with assertive people can be challenging if you feel intimidated easily, but assertive people are the best people to work with as they create fewer challenging situations. Here are some strategies that you can use to effectively collaborate with them:

Establish clear communication: Assertive individuals value clear and direct communication. Make sure that your communication is straightforward, concise, and focused on the issues at hand.

Focus on solutions: When discussing problems or issues, focus on finding solutions rather than dwelling on the negatives. Assertive people are goal-oriented and prefer to focus on actions that can be taken to improve the situation.

Be confident: Assertive individuals respect confident and decisive actions. Be confident in your decisions and trust your instincts. Think about the pros and cons of the decision and present them as such. This will help you earn their respect and build a strong working relationship.

Listen actively: Assertive individuals have strong opinions and ideas. Listen actively to their perspectives and show that you value their input. Consider their ideas and opinions, even if you don't agree with them. You can do that by acknowledging what was said and then agreeing/disagreeing by saying what you want to convey.

Be respectful: Assertive people appreciate respect and professionalism. Treat them with respect and avoid belittling or dismissing their ideas or opinions. Acknowledge their strengths and contributions and show your appreciation for their hard work.

#girlconsultant lifehacks:

Working with an assertive colleague: Remember that assertive people can be strong allies and valuable members of your team. By establishing clear communication, focusing on solutions, being confident, listening actively, and being respectful, you can effectively collaborate with them and achieve your shared goals.

My Favorite Boss of All Time

The only time I had an assertive boss was my small stint at one of the biggest German fashion brands, before the COVID-19 pandemic hit. Then, I got let go because I was on the innovations team and obviously not business survival-mode relevant. Miriam was the coolest person I have ever worked with. She was the one who really wanted to hire me for her team. Of course, I was excited to join, even though

I took a pay cut and had to move towns, because knowing her was so worth it.

When we worked together, there was mutual respect for our work, and our skill sets complemented each other. When she told me things, I would listen, and vice versa. Her ideas were brilliant. She was in charge of coming up with the digitization projects, and I was in charge of making them happen. It was a perfect duo. The way she managed every situation was incredible, with so much understanding and acceptance. Once, I remember I called her "babes" by accident, and she reacted in a cool and fun way and didn't feel offended or have the feeling that I disrespected her.

On another occasion, I saw her struggling with an Excel sheet, and as a consultant, I obviously know Excel with my eyes closed. I told her straight up: "Come on, let me do this for you. It will be quicker. Tell me what you need and I will have it ready for you in no time." She was delighted with my initiative. She moved her chair to make room for me at the keyboard and told me what she needed. I went to work and when she came back from getting a coffee, it was all done. She thanked me and we proceeded with work. I was happy to make her happy, and she was happy she did not have to do Excel.

> She could have been offended that I did not think she was good enough in Excel, but instead, she was happy to accept help and acknowledge it was not her strength. Although I only worked for her for a short time, this is who I always think of emulating when I am in a position to be a leader at work.

Passive-aggressive

Passive-aggressive behavior, according to Collins English Dictionary, relates to a personality that harbors negative (and at times even aggressive) emotions while behaving in a calm or detached manner.[23] It means that the feelings and emotions that this person has may be intense, but they are not expressed as such. There is a disconnect between the person's thoughts and actions.

There is a spectrum of passive-aggressive people: some might be more at the passive end while others are more at the aggressive end. Those individuals who lean toward the passive end tend to indirectly express their negative emotions toward others, often projecting their inner aggression onto them as a coping mechanism. In contrast, those toward the aggressive end are more inclined to engage in acts of sabotage or covert behaviors behind other peoples' backs (those who gossip a lot and create difficult situations for you).

---

[23] "Definition of 'passive-aggressive'", *Collins Dictionary*, 23.10.2024, https://www.collinsdictionary.com/dictionary/english/passive-aggressive

How do they respond to criticism?	"Sorry." (But thinks: "Pff. But it is not my fault!")
How do they engage with their environment and peers?	They appear cooperative while purposely doing things to annoy and disrupt others. They use sarcasm, stubbornness, and subtle sabotage to get even and avoid direct confrontation.
What do they think?	"You are not OK; I am (not) OK."

What is their body language like?	"Fine . . . whatever" attitude and body language; uses facial expressions that do not match how they feel (e.g., smiling when angry). Often crosses their arms.
How are they perceived by their peers?	Having difficulty acknowledging their anger, they feel inward negative emotions and have a low tolerance for frustration.

How to work with passive-aggressive people:

Working with passive-aggressive people can be frustrating and challenging, but it is important to find ways to collaborate effectively. Here are some strategies you can use to manage passive-aggressive behavior and work with these individuals:

Be direct: Passive-aggressive people often express their anger or frustration in indirect ways.

Acknowledge their feelings: Passive-aggressive behavior is often a sign of underlying anger or frustration. Acknowledge their feelings and try to understand the root cause of their behavior. You can use the "sandwich approach"—a communication technique used to provide feedback or address an issue while softening the impact of criticism (so they won't sabotage your career!). It involves sandwiching constructive feedback or acknowledgment between a positive opener and final empathetic positively affirming statements.

Focus on behavior, not personality: Passive-aggressive behavior can be frustrating, but it is important to focus on the behavior rather than the person. After all, it is difficult to change someone, but you want to make managing them better for both your well-being and the longevity of your project with them. Be clear about what behaviors are acceptable and which are not, and hold them accountable for their actions.

Use "I" statements: When communicating with passive-aggressive individuals, use "I" statements to express your feelings and opinions. This can help to avoid triggering defensive or aggressive behavior. Focus on the solution and the areas you find agreement, instead of disagreement.

Seek support: If you feel overwhelmed or unable to manage the behavior, seek support from a trusted colleague, supervisor, or HR representative. They can help mediate the situation and provide guidance on how to manage the behavior.

#girlconsultant lifehacks:

Working with a passive-aggressive colleague: Remember that passive-aggressive behavior can be a sign of deeper underlying issues, such as fear, anxiety, or low self-esteem. By being direct, acknowledging their feelings, focusing on behavior, using "I"

statements, and seeking support when needed, you can effectively manage the behavior and work with passive-aggressive individuals to achieve your goals. Their behavior has nothing to
do with you or your personality; it has everything to do with them.

The One Boss Who Was Never Honest

I once had a passive-aggressive boss. He suddenly appeared because of a reorganization of the departments, and then there he was and I had to work with him. His name was Giorgio. First, he never really took the time to get to know me. He would listen more to what other people said about me than to what I told him myself. He used to gossip and make up stories about me behind my back, and then my colleagues would call me and tell me what he said about me. One day, I told him that I was not challenged enough on the project, and I wanted to get involved in more things. He would always say, "Yes, sure, I will do something about that," but nothing ever happened.

I studied supply chain and worked on a lot of production-related topics, and one day, he was telling me how he needed someone with supply chain knowledge for a project. I then said, "Hello, it is me. I have a lot of experience in that." He was surprised and looked at me all puzzled and said, "You? Really?" I continued to make my case and tell him about my experiences, and mind you, by that time, we had already been working together for around three months.

Passive-aggressive types of people (especially the ones toward the aggressive end) are difficult to spot because you can never really tell what they are thinking. I always tried to be assertive and polite around this particular boss, but I eventually moved projects to find a new more assertive and useful boss to work with.

Aggressive:

According to Collins English Dictionary: Aggressive behavior has a quality of anger and determination that makes people ready to attack.[24] At work, aggressive people may behave in a forceful way because they are very eager to succeed, but you could equate their behavior as dominant.

---

[24] "Definition of 'aggressive'", *Collins Dictionary*, 23.10.2024, https://www.collins-dictionary.com/dictionary/english/aggressive

How do they respond to criticism?	"What?! No, I did not" (pretending to be innocent).
How do they engage with their environment and peers?	They like to attack or ignore others and others' opinions in favor of their own. They feed into others' fears by being ruthless and seeing themselves as the most important.
What do they think?	"You are not OK; I am OK."

What is their body language like?	They speak in a strong, loud voice, with threatening gestures and intimidating posture. They maintain direct eye contact, hold the head still while listening and talking, and often cross their arms. They interrupt and like to hear themselves speak more than others.
How are they perceived by their peers?	They need to win, are dominant, are easily frustrated, and have low tolerance.

How to work with aggressive people:

Aggressive people are more common as you ascend the career ladder, particularly among CEOs and senior management personnel. Working with aggressive people can be challenging, but it is important to find ways to collaborate effectively and avoid letting such behavior hinder your progress and teamwork. Here are some strategies you can use to manage aggressive behavior and work with aggressive individuals:

Set clear boundaries: It is important to set clear boundaries and expectations for how you want to be treated. Communicate these boundaries clearly and calmly and be firm about enforcing them. Be assertive about these boundaries and defend them, even if they do not like it.

Stay calm: Aggressive behavior can be triggered by a number of factors, such as stress or frustration. If you remain calm and composed, it can help to de-escalate the situation and prevent it from escalating further. Do not use loud or contentious language with them—they will feel attacked, often leading to a defensive response.

Avoid confrontation: Confrontation can often escalate the situation and make things worse. Instead of reacting aggressively, take a step back and try to understand the underlying issues that are causing the behavior. This is often difficult because these types of people like being aggressive and getting all worked up. Again, you do not want to change their personality, but by making them feel respected, you are more likely to avoid difficult situations and find a resolution.

Focus on the problem: When dealing with aggressive people, try to focus on the problem at hand, rather than the person. Be objective and analytical, and work together to find solutions that work for everyone.

Seek support: If you feel threatened or unsafe, seek support from a trusted colleague, supervisor, or HR representative. They can help mediate the situation and provide guidance on how to manage the behavior.

#girlconsultant lifehacks:

Working with an aggressive colleague: Remember that aggressive behavior is often a symptom of deeper underlying issues, such as stress, anxiety, or frustration. By staying calm, setting clear boundaries, focusing on the problem, and seeking support when needed, you can effectively manage the behavior and work with aggressive individuals to achieve your goals.

The Aggressive Client

I once had a client, Daniel, who I would say was quite aggressive. It was impossible to build a trusting relationship with him. Since he was "the client" and I was "the consultant," I tried to keep a professional atmosphere, but since he was paying my bill, I did not really complain to my boss about his behavior. He had these random outbursts and got really loud if he did not understand my Excel analysis, for example, or if the PowerPoint slide was not pretty enough. I mean, his behavior had nothing to do with me but everything to do with him. I tried to close the project as soon as possible and move on with my life, as in move on to a new project. Being exposed for too long to such people is not good for anyone's mental health.

Becoming assertive: A quick how-to

To become an assertive #girlconsultant, here are several practical steps that you can take:

- **Start with self-reflection:** Take the time to understand your needs, goals, and values. Reflect on your communication style and identify areas where you could be more assertive.

- **Practice effective communication:** Assertiveness relies heavily on effective communication. Work on being clear and direct when expressing your wants, needs, positions, and boundaries to others.

- **Learn to say "no":** Saying "no" can be difficult for many people, but it is an essential part of being assertive. Practice setting boundaries and saying "no" in a respectful and firm manner.

- **Use "I" statements:** When expressing your needs and feelings, use "I" statements rather than "you" statements. This can help prevent others from feeling attacked or defensive.

- **Practice active listening:** Assertiveness also involves actively listening to others. Show that you are listening by using appropriate body language and asking clarifying questions.

- **Use positive self-talk:** Assertiveness can be challenging, especially if you are used to being passive or aggressive. Practice using positive self-talk to build confidence and reinforce your assertive behaviors.

- **Seek support:** If you are struggling to become more assertive, seek support from a therapist or coach. They can help you develop strategies for improving your assertiveness and provide ongoing support and encouragement.

The power of being an assertive person

Now you may ask: "But Tanja, this is a book about consulting, so why are you encouraging me to become an assertive person in general?" You are absolutely correct, this is a book about consulting. But think back to Alex—the consultant at the beginning of the chapter. Is she likely to progress with her projects or feel content with her work if she does not develop her assertiveness? Very unlikely, right?

Being assertive is a skill to communicate effectively, build trust, resolve conflicts, and achieve goals, and girlfriend, these four points are major parts of life in general. But as mentioned earlier in this chapter, no one can ALWAYS be assertive in all areas of life.

When I started working, I was trying to find someone to aspire to, to emulate their great qualities so I could elevate my career. It was hard to find someone I truly looked up to, especially because there were so few women role models. And there were also no male bosses who were particularly cool or assertive or confident, where I found myself thinking, "I want to be like this person." No one around me was really assertive. Becoming assertive is the first step to being your own role model.

Now you know what assertiveness type you are, and you also know how to spot the assertiveness types of other people.

tl;dr

- Assertiveness is a crucial social skill that involves effective communication while respecting others' thoughts and wishes.

- Being assertive means expressing your needs, wants, and boundaries clearly and respectfully, without being aggressive or passive.

- Embracing assertiveness leads to greater self-confidence and reduced anxiety in stressful situations.

- Understand the different levels of assertiveness (passive, assertive, passive-aggressive, and aggressive) to better navigate interpersonal dynamics at work and in personal relationships.

- Strategies for working with passive individuals include encouraging them to speak up, providing clear expectations, and offering support and acknowledgment.

- Deal with passive-aggressive individuals by using clear communication, addressing underlying issues, and staying focused on the problem rather than the person.

- Effectively collaborate with aggressive individuals by setting boundaries, staying calm, and focusing on solutions.

- Becoming assertive involves self-reflection, effective communication, learning to say "no," using "I" statements, active listening, and positive self-talk.

- Assertiveness is crucial in consulting, facilitating effective communication, building trust, resolving conflicts, and achieving goals.

- The relationship between assertiveness and confidence, while related, is distinct, but aspiring to be both assertive and confident can lead to success and fulfillment in personal and professional life.

CHAPTER 9

Things You'll Learn in Consulting (Your Hard Skills Toolbox)

I n the fast-paced and dynamic world of consulting, professionals need a diverse set of skills to thrive and deliver
exceptional value to their clients. As a successful #girl-
consultant, you must not only possess technical expertise but
also excel in interpersonal and problem-solving abilities. This
combination of soft skills, which pertain to personal attributes
and communication, along with hard skills, which are specific
to the domain—such as research skills, strategic and analytical thinking, and technological proficiency—will allow you
to effectively navigate complex projects and deliver impactful
results. In this chapter, we focus on hard skills.

At first sight, these skills may look like a lot, but there is
an art to everything, and these are skills that will make your
day-to-day at work easier for the rest of your life. You do not
believe me? Send me a message on your tenth work anniversary,
wherever you are in the world, and whatever job you might be
doing, and let me know if I was right. I would be delighted to
hear from you!

I could list all the skills that you will learn during your consulting career, but I am focusing on the four main hard skills (research skills, strategic thinking, analytical thinking, and technological proficiency). These are the ones you will learn to master and the things you will be able to fall back on as you progress in your career. In other words, these four skills will serve you the most in the future. First, here is the way to approach thinking about these skills:

- If you have the skills, then you are already a great match for this industry, and you'll develop them even further.

- If you do not yet have these skills, you will learn them and these will take you far, because when you leave consulting, you will have a whole range of skills that transfer to other employment opportunities.

- If you are nervous about not having these skills yet, do not worry. You are a smart cookie; you will be up to speed in no time.

As for me, I learned so many things that now, just like a Swiss army knife, I can do everything and anything. I can calculate a business case, which requires industry knowledge, data analysis, and Excel skills, and I can also lead a design-thinking workshop, which requires presentation skills, critical thinking, and creativity. I love learning, especially new skills. And I also believe that knowing 80 percent of a lot of different things makes life so much more fun than just knowing a few skills perfectly. Now you might think about the saying: "Jack of all trades and the master of none." But did you know this particular quote is thought to have ended originally with: "but oftentimes better than a master of one"?

Hard skills versus soft skills

Hard skills acquired through education and training form the foundation of a career, enabling you to secure entry-level positions and gain credibility in your chosen field. In contrast, soft skills, like communication and leadership, become increasingly vital as we advance in our professional lives, fostering effective collaboration, adaptability, and relationship-building. Soft skills empower us to navigate complex dynamics, excel in leadership roles, and remain invaluable in a rapidly changing work environment. A combination of both hard and soft skills is key to achieving long-term success and career growth.

If you don't know, now you know:

Hard Skills versus Soft Skills: Hard skills acquired through education and training form the foundation of a career, enabling you to secure entry-level positions and gain credibility in your chosen field. In contrast, soft skills, like communication and leadership, become increasingly vital as we advance in our professional lives, fostering effective collaboration, adaptability, and relationship-building.

Hard skills are things you learn that let you tackle job-specific duties and responsibilities. Hard skills can be learned through courses, university, and most importantly, on the job. These skills are typically quantifiable and measurable, and they can be applied to perform specific tasks or functions within a particular domain. In consulting, the hard skills you learn have such a large range that you are able to do any job in the business field that you wish.

Research skills

Research skills are the ability to efficiently gather, assess, and interpret information from various sources. These skills involve conducting thorough investigations, formulating research questions, and employing critical thinking to analyze data and draw meaningful conclusions. With research skills, you can navigate databases and online resources adeptly, ensuring the accuracy and credibility of the information you use. Being proficient in research enables you to make informed decisions, support arguments, and stay well-informed in both academic and professional endeavors.

If you don't know, now you know:

Research skills are the ability to efficiently gather, assess, and interpret information from various sources.

You have probably written a lot of research papers at university and would now call yourself proficient. However, in my experience, research for work hits differently. Technically, it is still going on the internet and looking for things, but sometimes it is difficult because of the specificity of the question. It may be related to the client that you are currently working for, or it may be related to a specific industry niche. It may also be a simple question on how to create a specific formula in Excel or create a master slide in PowerPoint.

I remember in school they always told us: there are no stupid questions. Unfortunately, as I had to learn quickly, that is not entirely true. Try not to ask your question if you can find the answer easily on the internet. Let me explain a little better: No one knows everything, so most of the time, if you ask someone for something, they will also go online, and type into a search engine exactly the question that you have just asked. You could have done that yourself, you catch my drift? There is also an official term for this: it is called an "askhole." Urban dictionary defines an askhole as an annoying individual who asks random questions with no substance or asks stupid questions without thinking.[25]

Given my experience in consulting, I would always advise that you do a 15- to 30-minute internet search (including current large language models of course) first before you ask someone, because chances are that they will also not know and will also refer you to the internet. If you cannot find your own answer, then say: "I have already looked online for 15 to 30 minutes." They will probably think about who else you can ask, if they don't know the answer and it cannot easily be found online.

---

[25] "Askhole", *Urban Dictionary*, 23.10.2024, https://www.urbandictionary.com/define.php?term=Askhole

How research skills are used in your job in consulting:

When you start a project, there are a lot of new things to learn. First, every company has their own abbreviations they use to run their business. Next, there are the industry specific abbreviations, and lastly, there are the project-specific abbreviations that at the beginning may throw you off because you do not know what they mean. With good research skills, you will definitely learn them faster.

Try to ask as many questions as you can during the first two weeks of the project. Take notes of what all the abbreviations mean and try not to ask them again too many times after those two weeks. In my experience, there is a two-week grace period for all the questions, to make sure you are onboarded and ready to be operational. After those two weeks, you can still ask questions, just be sure to ask them to someone on your level, or if there is no one, then one level above.

As mentioned in chapter 7, the proposal and the statement of work are the documents that the client signed to start the project. I recommend you read through them thoroughly and make sure you understand them. If you know what the project objectives, timeline, approach, and tasks are, you can more easily go to your project leader and ask if you can take over one specific area. She will be happy that she does not have to guide you in everything, and you can be sure you are not left with unimportant tasks but will actually learn and add value. When it comes to doing the tasks that lead to the deliverables listed in the statement of work, you will probably need your research skills to figure out how to do some of them. Even if you only have a rough idea about how to tackle something, it is better than starting the discussion with your boss with zero knowledge.

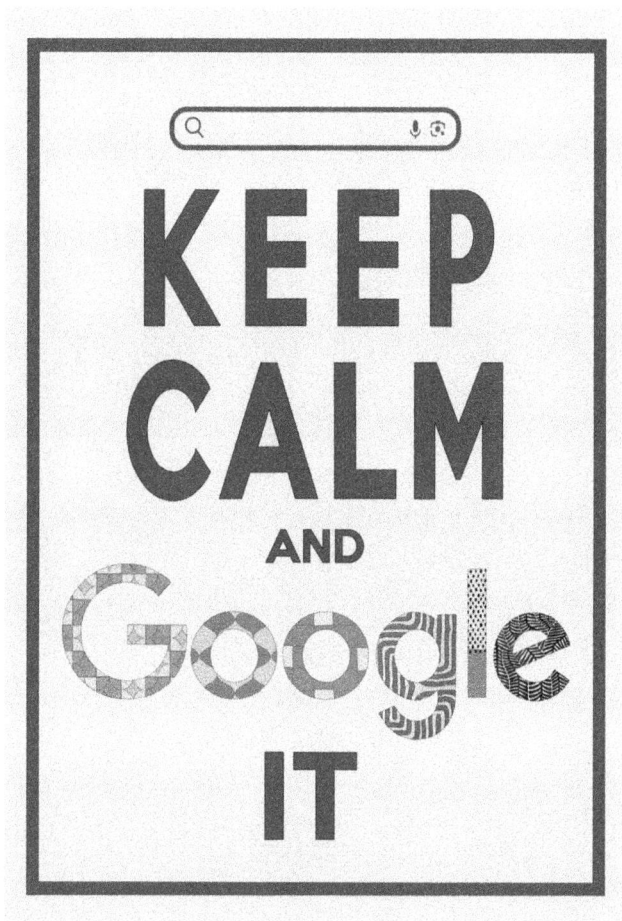

How is this skill useful in your future career:

In my experience, there are two types of people: the ones who research literally EVERYTHING, and those who do not. I definitely belong to the latter group. Growing up, I had a dad who always knew everything we were supposed to know for school, because he is just that smart, so it never really motivated me to do my own research. In consulting, however, because I was all grown-up, there was no one who was all-knowing and could explain, nor anyone who had the patience and time to explain everything. So, in the end, all I was left with was to really get in there and learn on my own.

Being able to organize yourself and dive deep into the details will help you to be more independent in basically every job you will have. With strong research abilities, you can gather relevant and reliable information, enabling informed decision-making and strategic planning. These skills empower you to stay up-to-date with industry trends, competitive analysis, and customer preferences, fostering innovation and adaptability. As a result, research skills not only bolster your credibility as a knowledgeable professional but also enable you to contribute significantly to your team's efficiency, productivity, and overall success.

The Time I Was a Manager and Someone on My Team Didn't Google It

The following story showcases one of my very first experiences as a new manager, with a girl named Sarah, who did not use Google, ChatGPT (which didn't exist back then), or any other form of research. She just asked me questions. All. The. Time.

It was Saturday and I was cleaning up the last bits and pieces from my twenty-fifth birthday party when my manager Alexandra called me. "I am staffing you on a project, and you will be the Project Manager; there is enough budget for three people," Alexandra said.

"OH MY GOD! That's amazing!" I shouted into the phone. "When do I start?"

"You start Monday," Alexandra stated calmly. "I am sending you an email with the people in your team. Contact them and onboard them ASAP."

"Excellent! I will do so," I replied.

I was so excited! I was going to have my own team!

I called the first person, a young woman who had recently joined the company. I was excited to be working with another woman and thought it was going to be terrific.

I helped her book her flights, and then a week later, she arrived on site. I soon realized it was not going to be as easy to work with her as I thought. Aside from the fact that she kept asking me my age, which I reluctantly told her, she then felt the need to remark: "How strange. You are only one day older than me."

"Yes, I am, and I have three years' experience in consulting," I said and politely smiled and continued working. Savage, I know.

I sat next to her so that she could ask questions. She was smart, no doubt about that, but she was used to being the young one, and she was used to being the star of every show.

One morning, she asked me for Excel assistance, which I agreed to.

"I want to look up something in this column," Sarah explained.

"Use a VLOOKUP," I suggested. "Do you know how to use the formula?"

"No, can you show me?" she asked.

With a nod, I took on the role of a patient guide. "Sure, let me walk you through it." I proceeded to walk her through each step.

Sarah's eyes brightened with understanding. "Oh, I see. Let me try that."

I told her to do it once herself, because I had to leave for a meeting. When I returned midday, she told me Excel was not working.

I looked at her Excel sheet, and I saw a lot of cells containing "#ref!" (which is an error message indicating a formula has been used incorrectly). The issue was not Excel; it was Sarah. So, I was a little disappointed. She just spent half a day trying to do two VLOOKUPs in Excel. I asked myself: "Why did she not consult Google on how to fix the errors? Or even YouTube?" There are usually so many explanation videos on how to do Excel.

Sarah was the kind of girl who would talk all day long. She would ask questions, make comments to herself, and have a war on silence. This went on and on. We were well into her fourth week on the project when I started getting more and more sleepy during the day. I could never finish anything properly without her chatting and asking questions beside me. I was young at the time, and I should have been more assertive, but I decided to avoid the conversation, and just sit in a different room. I did not want to do all my work at night in the hotel room on those tiny desks, with the smallest lamp in the world.

Truthfully, Excel issues aside, this job was not for Sarah. She was nervous every day. Her face was always bright red with anxiety when she came back from a meeting, hands shaking, and she would reach into her bag, pull out a little Tupperware box filled with broken-up chocolate and eat a piece. It was clear that she had difficulties adapting and going with the flow. The day before she told me she was quitting, my other colleagues and I had a lengthy discussion on how we could help her survive this job, because it looked like she was barely managing.

In retrospect, she should have had more initiative and Googled more things before she came to me, and I should have told her earlier to please stop asking questions and try to research things on her own first. I should have set a boundary and told her that she had 30 minutes every morning to ask me any question she wanted, and then, no more questions. I needed to do my own work. I am telling you how I felt from a manager's perspective, because only when I became a manager did I understand how important it is to do your own research and not ask everyone around you questions all the time. You have to be able to take the initiative to look into things yourself and be well-versed in researching what you do not know.

Strategic thinking

Strategic thinking is the ability to think about the impact of something at a high level and for the long-term. In consulting, strategic thinking refers to the ability to analyze complex business problems, assess the broader context, and develop long-term plans or strategies to achieve organizational goals.

If you don't know, now you know:
Strategic thinking is the ability to think about the impact of something at a high level for the long-term.

Here is a simple example I think everyone can relate to: Let's say your life goal is to earn a lot of money. Then, being strategic about it, you would look for a high-paying job or a job that is a good stepping stone to a job that would pay a lot in the future. You are thinking long-term, and you are making decisions that will help you reach your goal. You continuously educate yourself and get a master's degree, maybe an MBA, because you know this will help you reach your goal. You might invest in getting your MBA at Harvard to get a bigger paycheck after you graduate. In this example, you are making a plan oriented toward achieving a personal goal or objective. In consulting, you would be advising the client on a proposed plan that would help them achieve their goal or objective.

How strategic thinking is used in your job in consulting:

We spoke about Strategy Consulting in chapter 2, and even if you do not end up in that department, you will still learn how to think strategically. Every project you are on has a strategic part. Here are some key aspects of strategic thinking in consulting:

Big picture perspective: Strategic thinking involves considering the larger context and understanding how various elements within and outside the organization interact. You need to grasp the organization's vision, mission, and long-term objectives to develop strategies that align with these overarching goals.

Anticipating and adapting to change: Strategic thinking involves anticipating future trends, industry disruptions, and changes in market dynamics. You should assess the potential impact of these changes on the client's business and help them adapt their strategies accordingly. This requires being proactive, flexible, and open to exploring new opportunities or adjusting plans as needed.

Risk assessment and mitigation: Strategic thinking involves assessing risks and uncertainties associated with different strategies or courses of action. You need to evaluate potential risks, consider risk-reward trade-offs, and develop mitigation strategies to minimize potential negative impacts on the client's business.

How this skill is useful in your future career:

One of the main benefits of learning how to think strategically, apart from the frameworks (such as Porter's Five Forces from chapter 6), is actually speaking the language of your counterpart. What I mean by this is being able to adjust what you are saying based on who you are speaking to. Not every person you interact with on a project needs the same level of detail or context. For example, you would not take the data analytics from your analysis and talk about individual numbers with a

CEO unless he explicitly asked for them. With the CEO, you would speak about the numbers in a broad sense, perhaps via a chart, illustrating what the numbers represent as a whole. You would discuss what impact these numbers have, and what they mean for her business. With a data analyst, on the other hand, you would open your spreadsheet and look at individual numbers; you would discuss how reliable these numbers are, where they are coming from, and if there are other numbers that you can use. With the data analyst you would really dive into the details, but with the CEO you would talk in broader, big picture terms.

As you climb the ranks of your career, you will speak to C-Level executives and directors sooner or later and you will notice that you have an advantage over people who have not had this kind of exposure to higher-level management. You will be versed in knowing what to talk about and at what level of detail. These skills will help you gain further visibility and credibility in any position, because you know what to say and share and how to say and share it.

Analytical thinking

On one side of the spectrum, we have strategic thinking (high-level, big picture) and on the other side of the spectrum, we have analytical thinking, which is more detail-oriented, yet they go hand in hand. Analytical thinking refers to the ability to collect, interpret, analyze, and evaluate information to understand patterns, solve problems, make informed decisions, and derive meaningful insights. These skills involve breaking down complex problems or situations into smaller components, examining relationships between variables, and drawing logical conclusions based on evidence and data.

If you don't know, now you know:

Analytical thinking refers to the ability to collect, interpret, analyze, and evaluate information to understand patterns, solve problems, make informed decisions, and derive meaningful insights.

Using the previous example of you trying to eventually make more money: you might use analytical thinking to analyze and evaluate whether getting a Harvard MBA is going to get you where you want to be. You would calculate your business case and see when the investment of the tuition can be recuperated by the higher-paying salary you would get after the MBA. You would also consider where you live, and if the network of Harvard alumni is better leveraged in the US, and if maybe the Institut Européen d'Administration des Affaires (INSEAD) alumni can be more useful in Europe. You catch my point?

How it is used in your job in consulting:

In consulting, we basically always problem solve. The whole concept is based on the fact that the client has an issue—no matter what issue—and the consultant finds a way of solving it. Different tools and skills are used to solve this issue, but analytical thinking is ALWAYS employed. Analytical thinking enables you to identify and define the correct problem, extract key information from the data available, make assumptions (if and when necessary), find one or more solutions, and finally, present it to the relevant stakeholders.

How this skill is useful in your future career:

Your analytical thinking skills will be so solid by the time you seek other employment that you will be confident in solving any and every problem that you are faced with. First, you will not be afraid of tackling it, regardless of how big or complex. Second, you will find a way to solve it by leveraging all of the other tools you now have in your toolbox, thanks to your prior career in consulting. You will be able to find the right data sources, analyze them, and find your way. You will be able to consolidate the data, look at it from a bird's-eye perspective, and communicate it to the stakeholders in a way that they will understand. This is not only transferable to business issues, but also to interpersonal issues. Imagine you are the head of a large team. There will be interpersonal, social, and community issues to face. With the help of your analytical mindset and the tools that you have at hand, you will also be able to solve these issues.

Technological proficiency

Proficiency in relevant software and tools is important for consultants to analyze data, manage projects, and deliver insights effectively. Without the right tools, you cannot calculate a business case or outline a strategy. Familiarity with project management software, data visualization tools, and industry-specific software is vital. Technology is advancing rapidly, and learning how to use the most common programs is key.

Technical skills are typically tangible and measurable, and they are often job-specific and directly related to the responsibilities and requirements of a particular profession or industry. Examples of technical skills can vary widely based on the field, ranging from computer programming, data analysis, and graphic design to video cutting and creative writing. In many professions, technical skills are complemented by other soft skills, such as communication, teamwork, and problem-solving to create a well-rounded and successful professional. Your technical skills are part of every resume, and you will most likely already have acquired many during your studies or on any internships you may have done. Consulting must-haves: proficiency with Excel, PowerPoint, Word, and Outlook, or the Google equivalents. Even if you don't have experience with these, you will learn them.

If you don't know, now you know:

Technical skills definition: Technical skills are typically tangible and measurable, and they are often job-specific and directly related to the responsibilities and requirements of a particular profession or industry.

Of those four, Excel and PowerPoint are probably the most important. These two core programs will make your life after consulting much easier. Even if you get a job in sales, and you only use customer relationship management (CRM) software, the minute you calculate a business case for the client or the cost of the product, you will take Excel out again and do it in a jiffy. When it comes to PowerPoint, you will learn how to build a compelling storyline, how to present a slide, and how to aggregate information on a slide. These skills are always good to have, no matter where you are later in life.

The IT technical skills you will acquire during consulting actually depend on the projects you choose to be staffed on. Sometimes different projects require technical skills that you do not have yet, but that you will probably learn while working. This may be specific program knowledge because the client uses SAP as their enterprise resource planning (ERP) software, or Salesforce as a CRM solution, and you are restructuring their sales organization. It may also be R statistical software or IBM's Statistical Package for the Social Sciences (SPSS) because a project you are on requires you to work on a statistical model with a more senior project member. Maybe it is also learning how to use Adobe Premiere, a video cutting software, because you had to cut a video for a client to present the vision of the project. While Excel and PowerPoint are technical skills that will likely be useful across any and all projects or clients, there are several others you may have to learn on the job to achieve the project objective.

If you don´t know, now you know:

ERP stands for enterprise resource planning. It is the software used to manage the main business processes of a company. Usually production data, company inventory, purchasing, finance data, HR, etc. are mapped in the ERP. The programs used vary depending on the industry the client is in. For example, in manufacturing, the most common ERP is SAP, which originally stood for Systems Applications and Products.

Excel as a core technical skill

Likely you used Excel at university, depending on what you studied. You may even know the basic Excel formulas (e.g., pivot table, VLOOKUPs, HLOOKUPs, sum-ifs, index matches, or VLOOKUP match). Even if you have never used these formulas, do not be afraid of them. Practice makes perfect. And, if you have no reason to use these formulas, you probably will not remember them. That is also fine because you just need to know what they do, and you can Google the rest.

I recommend always using formulas. If you are doing a one-time simple analysis, then use formulas if it makes sense. If you are doing reporting and using your Excel on a weekly basis, automate as much as you can with the help of macros. It might take you a day to figure everything out and to implement it, but any day afterward, it will save you time. Do not be afraid of Excel; the more you use it, the better and more efficient you will get and the more you will be able to automate. It will be your friend once you learn it intimately.

If you don't know, now you know:

In Excel, a macro is a rule or command that specifies how a certain input should be mapped to a replacement output. It is a small program that is written in Visual Basic (programming language) and can be executed indefinitely. Use it to automate repetitive tasks.

Another recommendation is to learn the shortcuts for Excel. They also save so much time. Find the most common ones and the ones I always use in the call out box.

If you don't know, now you know: The most common Excel shortcuts

Action	Shortcut
Write/edit a cell	(F2)
Fix a cell	(F4)
Move forward and backward	TAB and SHIFT+TAB
Going to the first cell and last cell, respectively	CTRL+Home and CTRL+End
Select an entire column and select an entire row, respectively	SHIFT+Space and CTRL+Space
Insert row or column	CTRL+SHIFT+ +
Delete row or column	CTRL+ -
Hide and unhide rows	CTRL+9 and CTRL+SHIFT+9
Insert a table	CTRL+L
Add filters	CTRL+SHIFT+L

Outsourcing Excel at All Costs?

The client asked a consultant from another team for some Excel calculations. The consultant, however, did not want to invest time to learn how to do some simple formulas, so she paid, out of her own pocket, a programmer in India to write her that formula. The next time the client asked if she could quickly change something on the formula sheet during a meeting, the consultant had to make up a reason to change the formula after the meeting instead.

This situation is wrong in so many ways. First, because of client data protection: Goodness knows what data she sent to that Indian programmer. Second, this consultant will have to work with Excel so many more times during her career, and she might lose credibility, and a lot of money, if she continues to hire someone to do the formulas for her.

Do not be like her. Learn Excel.

PowerPoint as a core technical skill

One ongoing joke in consulting is that the managing director scribbles something incomprehensible on a piece of paper, or a whiteboard, and tells the analyst to make a slide out of it. Then the analyst takes out his magnifying glass, has a look and takes a wild guess on what the slide should look like. Once finished, the slide is sent to the managing director, and comes back with a "plsfix," because it is probably not what they had envisioned (since no one can interpret the original drawing but them).

To save everyone some time, most slides are based on templates. For example, if you want to make three points, then you choose a slide already designed with that in mind. Or, if you would like to create a list of things, or present the outcomes of a graph, or depict a causality, take an already created template with the company branding and add your points to the slide. Or take already existing slide decks that you like and change the contents so you are not spending too much time designing the slide and can focus your energy more on the content.

Back in the day, you were not allowed to use any shadows or animations on the slides. Colors were not supposed to be bright, and the slide setup was always the same. This has changed since the world has become more visual. As consulting companies pride themselves on being innovative and forward thinking, they also have to create good visuals.

Go to girlconsultant.com and click on the shop link. With these at hand, your slides will look stunning!

How You Should NOT "PlsFix"

It was a Thursday around 4 p.m. I was going to Italy for the weekend, because I was on a project in Switzerland and Italy is closer to Switzerland than Düsseldorf, where I lived. I was ready to leave when my manager scribbled something on the whiteboard. It was some sort of arrow from left to right, getting bigger, showing a step-by-step approach.

I had already asked him to explain the slide to me several times, when he kept repeating: "Do you know what slide I mean? The one with the step-by-step approach?"

I was too afraid to say, *No, I still do not*, so I said: "Yes, sure, I understand."

"Can you finish this slide for tomorrow morning?" he asked.

"Sure, I can," I replied.

What a mistake.

Imagine . . . I had no clue what he wanted from me. I took a picture of the scribbles on the whiteboard and when everyone left by 5 p.m. to catch their flights home, I sat in the project car, ready to go to Italy. Also, this is a typical case of "how did I get here?" by yours truly. I did NOT think this journey through. I thought, I will take a Redbull and drive through the night.

I was nearly through Switzerland when I just could not keep my eyes open anymore. It was dark and since in Switzerland the maximum speed you are allowed to drive is 120km/h, there was no adrenaline keeping me awake. I pulled into the next rest stop to take a break. I was so tired that I decided to take a nap. I reclined in the driver seat, took out my jacket, and heated the car a little so that I would not be that cold. I woke up an hour later shivering because the jacket was not enough to sleep in. I did this another three or four times, until I looked at how many hours I still had to drive. I decided to hit the road again. I filled up the tank, got three Redbulls just in case, and started my way to Italy.

It was around 7 a.m. when I realized I had not finished that slide. So I pulled up to the next rest stop, had a good Italian coffee, took out my laptop, and started designing that slide in PowerPoint. Needless to say, it was a complete disaster. I mean, my slide looked like some five-year-old had drawn it in kindergarten. Despite that, I was somehow proud of my guesswork and what I had done in a carpark in Italy, with only four hours of sleep. I sent it around noon on Friday and continued on my way to Italy.

The weekend was amazing, obviously; I was in Italy! On my way back, I started my trip on Sunday morning to get a good night's sleep before Monday. But upon arrival in the office on Monday morning, my boss was so mad at me, he was barking: "Your slide was so bad, I spent the whole of Friday afternoon redoing it!"

"Oh, I am sorry," I replied.

Because of this slide, my manager gave me a bad review for my performance on the project. After this, the tasks I had were practically non-existent. Everyone basically just waited for me to roll off the project. I am not going to lie; this is a clear sign of bad leadership. In retrospect, my boss knew I was going to Italy, and if he spent a whole afternoon on that slide, did he really expect me to do it in one night? With more experience, I could now do that slide in probably 30 minutes but back then it was a struggle.

So: do not be like me. Do not say yes to everything. I would have gotten away with saying: "Listen, I am on the road the whole night. I cannot deliver it to you in the morning. Can someone else do it?"

> Or I should have said: "Listen, I do not know what template you are talking about. Can you please share it with me, and please expect me to deliver it tomorrow evening, or Monday afternoon." I should have just said that and either not delivered anything at all or negotiated myself some more time so that I could ask a colleague to check my work instead of delivering something really bad.

How to go the extra mile using PowerPoint by being detail-oriented

We are all different. Some of us are very detail-oriented, giving 100 percent to whatever we do, and some are big picture (80:20) people. However, it does not really matter what kind of person you are; presentation in consulting is everything. A cake appears 100 times more delicious if it looks amazing. A person looks more competent if she is dressed well. The contents of a slide seem more accurate if the slide looks good.

With PowerPoint slides, the saying always goes: everyone criticizes what they can. This means that the easiest thing to b**** about is if the slides look messy, the boxes are not aligned, and/or there is a typo. It makes most people feel superior and good about themselves to point out things that are not correct or look sloppy.

Especially at the beginning, you will make a better impression if your slides do not look like a hot mess. Before sending the first draft to your manager, be sure to check off every item on the checklist I've included. "First draft" is usually code for sending a finished version of your document over. Do not send over half-baked things; you will simply have to explain too much. Finish it as much as you can and then have her add the finishing touches.

Checklist for Great Slides

- All boxes are aligned.
- If there are repeating elements on multiple consecutive slides, make sure they are in the same place from one slide to the next, so they do not jump when flipping back and forth between the slides quickly.
- Spell check is complete.
- The footer and page numbers are in the same place on every slide.
- The owner of the document is shown as you or your company.
- The colors used are either neutral or are from the client's or your company's brand.
- The font size and font type are the same from slide to slide.
- The spacing between the lines looks good.

#girlconsultant lifehacks: Bonus skill!
The Art of Notetaking

Taking notes and synthesizing the important: You may think that taking notes is not that big of a deal, because you are proficient in it already. You have taken notes at university and you are really good at it. Maybe you also have a quick grasp of things and never need to write anything down. If the latter is you, then kudos to you for not needing to write things down; however, when you are just starting off, there will be at least one senior person asking you why you do not write things down. These people often think you are not taking things seriously, because how can someone remember all the details? My recommendation would be to take a small notebook and write the important things down, no matter what.

Additionally, I recommend you do not take a laptop and stenograph every word as it is said. (Unless you are writing a blog or a book and want to record some bits of the conversation!) A laptop also puts a barrier between you and your counterpart; this may hinder a good conversation and may make the other person think that you may be doing something else. As an example, I once had a senior managing director who was so good at multitasking, he could interview candidates and write emails at the same time. Later the interviewee told me she thought it was quite rude, because clearly the managing director was writing something on the laptop, and she felt he was not paying attention to her. I had not considered that perspective before. I cannot remember if she got hired or not, but I do remember that while she was being interviewed, I received an email from that senior managing director on a business topic.

tl;dr

- Strong research skills are essential for gathering and analyzing relevant information in consulting.

- Google is your best friend for finding answers before asking unnecessary questions.

- Strategic thinking involves analyzing complex business problems and developing long-term plans aligned with client goals.

- Analytical thinking is crucial for problem-solving and deriving meaningful insights.

- Technological proficiency, especially in software like Excel and PowerPoint, is vital in consulting.

- Embracing new technologies and tools will help you stay ahead in the industry.

- Research, strategic thinking, analytical thinking, and technological proficiency are valuable skills for success in consulting.

CHAPTER 10

Things You'll Learn in Consulting (Your Soft Skills Toolbox)

Your Interpersonal Toolbox is one of the hardest ones to build, but it is also the most gratifying (in my opinion). For hard skills, you sit down, you learn the theory, you practice the skill, and then you perfect it. With interpersonal skills, you learn the theory and then you practice, and you practice, and then you practice some more. It takes a lot of experience and self-reflection to really have a refined toolbox, and that is because interpersonal skills all have to do with people and relationships, and these things can be complex. But you already knew this . . . you are human, after all.

As for myself, I am still learning, observing, and refining my interpersonal skills. Although the road is long and there will always be room for improvement, you are on the right track, and consulting is the right playground for that. Because there are ever-changing clients, internal teams, and topics, you will have plenty of chances to refine your soft skills.

In this chapter, I highlight six main interpersonal skills: communication, how to take and ask for feedback, presentation skills, problem-solving, building relationships, and how to network and why. Each of these you will practice and refine in your first two years of consulting. This list is obviously not exhaustive, and there are many more things that you can (and will) learn, but these are, from my point of view, the most important ones to be successful in consulting and any future career.

Communication

Communication is the fundamental process of exchanging information, thoughts, ideas, and feelings between individuals or groups. It encompasses various modes, including verbal, non-verbal, and written expressions, as well as active listening. Skillful communication promotes collaboration, resolves conflicts, and fosters empathy and understanding, building strong connections between people and contributing to personal and collective growth.[26]

If you don´t know, now you know:

Communication is the fundamental process of exchanging information, thoughts, ideas, and feelings between individuals or groups. It encompasses various modes, including verbal, non-verbal, and written expressions, as well as active listening.

---

[26] Adler, Ronald B., Lawrence B. Rosenfeld, and Russell F. Proctor. *Interplay: The Process of Interpersonal Communication*. 14th ed., Oxford University Press, 2018. 77.

How communication is used in your consulting career:

Effective communication is a cornerstone of success in consulting, serving as the bridge that connects you with clients, team members, and stakeholders. In the dynamic realm of consulting, communication skills are essential for understanding clients' needs, extracting vital information, and building trust. Whether it involves asking for information, presenting findings, or facilitating workshops, adept communication empowers you to navigate challenges with finesse and cultivate enduring client relationships.

One of my favorite bosses, Igor, said this to me when I asked him what skills he learned in consulting: "I learned that soft skills are much more important than hard skills, because they make you, you. I also learned that you have to listen to people, more than talk to them." Soft skills, such as communication, empathy, and emotional intelligence, play a significant role in defining a person's character and interactions with others. These skills help you navigate various situations, build meaningful relationships, and showcase your true self.

How communication is useful in your future career:

Effective communication starts with assertiveness (which we discussed in chapter 8). If you see assertiveness as a basis for good communication, you are already further than most people in life. The more and better you communicate, the easier it is to live your life because fewer things are left up to interpretation or "reading between the lines." When you say what you mean, it is better for everyone, especially you.

I once heard that the older you get, the more keys on the piano you will be able to play. This means that in different situations, you will communicate, react, and behave differently. You are a different person when you are out with your friends, versus when you are with your parents, versus when you are with your boss. You are still authentically you, but your communication is so nuanced that depending on the situation, you can play a different key. Learning all the different keys is difficult, but thanks to the ever-changing environment in consulting, you can practice and play around until you find the right way to communicate in every situation.

As the world grows more accepting of diversity and inclusiveness, we need to communicate more with each other to empathize and understand another person's point of view. Considering diverse viewpoints is also useful in problem-solving.

Take the image below. These five people are all looking at the same problem. However, as they have all had different experiences in life, they look at the problem from different angles. Communication is necessary to understand the other person's point of view to solve the problem from every angle. This is what makes good teams, creates an appreciative work environment, and fuels innovation.

Trial and Error Until Assertiveness Came Around

As you know from chapter 4, I moved around on various different projects with new clients and completely new teams. This enabled me to try out different communication styles. Each new project, I could practice and perfect the first impression I wanted my teammates to have of me. I wanted people to see me as charismatic, reliable, respected, and confident. I wanted people to see me as someone who knew what she was talking about. This took quite some time, and I went through several iterations. One of my iterations was trying to present myself more like the men do, because if they get respected and I act like them, I would too.

I remember I had just started a project, which I took over from another woman who left the project crying because she got hit on by the project leader on the client side. She suffered through sexual harassment and left because of it. It was a manufacturing company, so there were very few women. The only women in the company were in HR or were the administrative assistants. So I started the project, and I took the role very seriously. I was going to have to "save" the project, as my boss put it.

I rocked up my first day in a suit and told myself I would be all serious, so that I appeared older and wiser, and so no one would be interested in me beyond being a colleague. I managed to be serious for about two weeks, but then my smiley and happy attitude came through, and I was back to being myself. By this time, I had figured out how to be myself outside of the important meetings, and then resume seriousness when we started to speak about business. This was when my "let's talk business" game face was born. You have to imagine: no smile, no jokes, a bit of a wrinkle between the eyebrows, eye contact, constant nodding, and "uh-hum" as a sign that I am listening attentively and I am giving you all the attention in the world. I really like this style of communication. I have the feeling that I am present, I am listening, all my brain cells are switched on, and there are important matters to discuss. I have kept this habit of being serious and focused when I need to show everyone else at the table that I am taking things seriously.

How to take and ask for feedback

What is feedback in communication? It is an honest response about someone's behavior, deliverable, or choice of words. It is, hopefully, guidance on what can be improved to meet a specific standard, expectation, or intended feeling. Asking for feedback is always a good idea; however not all feedback is good feedback. This is a lesson that is especially close to my heart, because as a woman, you are always "too" something. Too tall, too short, too ugly, too pretty, too much makeup, not enough makeup, too fat, too thin, too professional, not professional enough—and the list goes on. However, feedback is still good for personal growth if it is the right kind of feedback about your professional performance (and not about your appearance or personality). There is always a time and place for feedback, and knowing how to ask and receive it is an art form.

If you don't know, now you know:

Feedback in communication is an honest response about someone's behavior, deliverable, or choice of words. It is, hopefully, guidance on what can be improved to meet a specific standard, expectation, or intended feeling.

When feedback should be asked and interpreted in your consulting career:

A good time to ask for feedback is around the midpoint of a project. If your project is longer than four to six months, I suggest asking for feedback after two to three months. This is to give you the opportunity to ask for feedback and then show your project manager that you can implement that feedback and improve during the time that remains.

If you ask for feedback, do it properly. Invite your project manager for a specific feedback meeting. Tell your manager that you would like to receive (and give) feedback, book a meeting room, and then go there prepared with notes about the areas you would like to improve in, but also areas where you think your boss could. Feedback goes both ways, and it may be scary at the beginning to give someone feedback, but as long as it is in a safe space, they will thank you for it. If you are giving someone feedback, without them asking you for that feedback first, set the tone and ask them the question: "May I give you feedback?" I have used this many times, and it may sound corny, but I have always been able to make my point by entering the conversation this way. Because what are they going to say: "No, you may NOT give me feedback"? That is bad management.

Assertiveness and receiving feedback

Remember when we spoke about the assertiveness types in chapter 8? When interpreting the feedback that is given to you, be sure to remind yourself who it is coming from and what underlying intention they may have:

Assertive:

You can be sure that an assertive person will give you an honest answer and that they will give you feedback on what benefits you. They will probably ask you who you want to be, who you look up to, and then give you feedback to help you achieve that goal. An assertive person is going to be very likely thinking from their own perspective of growth and have genuine interest in seeing you succeed. They would want you to grow in the same way they would if they were in your position. That person would also admit if something is out of scope or beyond their comfort zone. Generally, assertive people have your best interests at heart. Their advice is good advice.

Passive:

Passive people usually see other people as superior, as they have lower self-esteem. They compare themselves with everyone all the time, as they probably compare themselves to you. They may be putting you on a pedestal if they see you as more successful than them in any sort of way: aesthetically, behaviorally, socially, etc. Thus, the feedback they give you could seem positive but also be unrealistic. The passive person will probably not be able to give you honest insights if they are viewing you with rose-colored glasses rather than seeing your performance in a more objective way, meaning their feedback will probably be all positive. Their feedback may boost your confidence, but in terms of really improving and knowing what to work on, they may not provide you with useful insights

Passive-Aggressive:

Passive-aggressiveness comes on a spectrum. These people can have both passive and aggressive tendencies. If the tendency is more toward passive, information might be withheld and non-genuine and will probably only be 30 percent useful for you. With more aggressive tendencies, this person may offer feedback that stems from a place of having ulterior motives. For example, you may tell this person about a promotion that you are striving for, and this person is then thinking of sabotaging your progress. The comments and the feedback will be formulated and delivered in a way that the sabotage is not obvious. You find the information they provide very useful, and since the delivery seems honest and helpful, it can give you potentially misleading cues, wrong information, or lead you to the wrong people. Thus, think twice before you follow advice from someone who is passive-aggressive.

Aggressive:

Aggressive individuals often express their feedback in an intense manner because they have strong concerns or expectations. Try to identify the underlying issues or motivations behind their aggression. Are they frustrated with a particular aspect of your work? Are there unresolved conflicts or pressures influencing their feedback? If the feedback is unclear or too emotionally charged to fully grasp, politely ask for specific examples or further clarification. This will help you gain a clearer understanding of their perspective, the specific areas they want you to address, and whether the concerns are valid and their feedback is relevant—or if it is really more about them and not at all about you.

How asking and receiving feedback is useful in your future career:

Good feedback helps us grow and refine our skills. We are constantly developing, and feedback belongs to the lifelong learning journey. Whenever we level up to the next job, position, or challenge in our life, it will be easier if we are honest with each other. For example, if, as a team lead, you ask for feedback from your team, it shows that you are human, want to improve, and want to be better for the people you lead. If you give honest feedback to your team, it will help them improve and develop their skills, which they will be very thankful for in the long run.

You may also find yourself in the position of giving feedback to someone who is above you in the hierarchy. This can help you create trust with the big bosses, because sometimes all they have are people who say "yes" to everything, because they are afraid to say anything else. If you have good rapport with your big bosses, they will rely on your honest opinion, and you can become a trusted confidante. Having someone like that as a confidante is positive, because they can also give you feedback and help you improve and reach higher positions, more money, more responsibility, and/or better work-life balance.

The Time I Took Some Random Colleague's Feedback and Became Passive

As you can see, you need to be careful on what to believe from whom, because some people just want to put you down to make themselves feel better. Here is a story of how I let myself be influenced at the beginning of my career. This is a gentle reminder to not be like me, but to do better.

It was at the end of my first project, and I had just finished my first six months in consulting, and I was looking for a new project. I had been working for a big client, one that also had projects in the logistics and supply chain department. We were going to build a control tower for them—a dashboard that consolidates all the data of the company with suggestions on what to do if the numbers are not correct. An example would be: There has been a promotion for shampoo in one area of the country, and the shampoo is sold out in that particular area. What do you do? The control tower would present you with the following ideas, with a numerical estimate of how much it would cost you: a) Send shampoos from other stores to the one where it is sold out; b) Produce more and re-stock; or c) Do nothing.

A senior manager had invited me to a workshop, to "sit in," and since I was very determined that my next project would be in supply chain, I SAID SOMETHING during the workshop. Can you imagine? I said something. I listened, and people were trying to figure something out, and I went up to the flip chart and gave an idea on how to solve it. People were shocked that I had the guts to stand up and say something, and I was shocked that people were shocked. It is a very uncomfortable feeling. I think I was probably sweating through my shirt, but no one noticed since I was wearing a blazer over it.

So, I said what I said, and it was a good idea, in my book, and then that workshop passed, and because I was trying to network and convince people that I should get promoted soon, I asked for feedback so that I would have a reason to talk to them. I asked this guy who was in the workshop that day for feedback. I remember that when he told me, we were standing in one of those cubicles—the ones that are gray and blend in with the carpet. And guess what he said? "You are too loud. Try listening more and not talking so much." It's like a textbook answer to an outspoken woman because she pushed her boundaries to say something in a meeting, and at the same time probably intimidated a lot of guys who didn't have the courage to say anything.

I should not have taken that advice, but I did.

My next project was in supply chain, but it was not the control tower project. I was trying to be the quieter one who listened, but for my manager's taste I was "TOO quiet." He said that I was not bringing any value to the project, because I didn't bring any ideas nor would I ever say anything useful. I had never heard this feedback before. I always brought value, but then I remembered that I had changed because the other person had told me to.

I was miserable, and I felt so useless, incompetent, and stupid. I was going on a downward spiral hoping

241

I could just disappear. But I could not; I had to show up for work every day, knowing what other people thought of me. It was the project in chapter 11, where I did not know how to create the slide and delivered something that had to be re-done. It was also the project where I had lost all my confidence, because in the end, no one gave me any more work to do, and I just sat around, not knowing where to go or who to talk to. It was also the project I was supposed to be doing project management, and then in the end did not "add value" because I was not "pushy enough" to get everyone to the team meetings on time.

The only way for me to get out of this situation was to change projects. To just leave and start fresh. That is the good thing about consulting—you can be four months in this situation that is getting worse, and then all of a sudden, you snap out of it. If you are not in consulting, you might be stuck with a team for YEARS. On the next project, I met one of my favorite bosses, Igor, and it was one of my best projects I ever worked on.

In conclusion, feedback is good, but always treat it like a suggestion. In the end you decide what you think is best for you. I really hit rock bottom during that project, because I did not stay true to who I was; I did not work on who I wanted to be, but on who everyone else wanted me to be.

Presentation skills

Presentation skills are the abilities and qualities necessary for creating and delivering a compelling presentation that effectively communicates information and ideas. They encompass what you say, how you structure it, and the materials you include to support what you say, such as slides, videos, or images. Presentation skills are something you have probably already practiced in school and university. Standing in front of people and presenting is going to become normal for you because presenting is like a muscle. The more you train, the stronger it becomes. In consulting, if you are on a project, you are usually presenting at least once a week, during the jour-fixe (the weekly meeting to update your client on project progress).

If you don't know, now you know:

Presentation skills are the abilities and qualities necessary for creating and delivering a compelling presentation that effectively communicates information and ideas. They encompass what you say, how you structure it, and the materials you include to support what you say, such as slides, videos, or images.

A presentation nearly always includes PowerPoint in consulting, so in theory you have something to look at and read from. From my experience, you make the most impact if you talk freely and follow these rules:

- Speak loudly, clearly, and at a slower than usual pace.
- Do not use "ems," "ahs," "yeahs," or "sos," nervous laughter, or any filler word/sound.
- Do not repeat words at the beginning of the sentence. Take a pause instead. (It is so hard, but very powerful.)
- Look at people when you speak, but do not get distracted.
- Stand in a normal, relaxed way. Do not be too fussy with your hands, but also do not be a robot. Bend your arms at 90 degrees, pretend you are holding a ball in front of your stomach. Move your hands to accentuate the things you are saying.

How presentation skills are used in your consulting career

During your career, presenting will become second nature, and consulting is an excellent playground in which to practice. During a project, you will probably have a presentation once or twice a week, either in the weekly jour-fixe meeting to update the customer on the progress of the project or the internal meeting to discuss the roadmap and immediate tasks. I encourage you to sign up for presentation training if there is any available and to really work on improving this skill. If you are a good presenter, people will listen to you and you will gain gravitas and visibility. With good presentation skills, it will be easier to get that promotion, get on new and exciting projects, and manage the stakeholders of your organization.

How presentation skills are useful in your future career:

Wherever you are later in life, a good presenter will always capture the audience (no matter how small) and will always get their point across. Even if you do not aspire to become a TV personality, somewhere along the line you will have to present and will want to be comfortable doing so. If you really know how to present, the stress before a presentation becomes minimal, because you are confident and know you will charm the audience. Whether it is to present something to a board meeting or at a school function for your children, knowing how to present well will help you.

Problem-solving

Problem-solving is the cognitive process of identifying, analyzing, and resolving challenges or issues to reach well-considered solutions. It involves the systematic and logical application of knowledge, skills, and creativity to overcome obstacles and achieve desired outcomes. Successful problem-solving empowers individuals to tackle complex situations with confidence, navigate through uncertainty, and arrive at practical and innovative solutions.

If you don't know, now you know:

Problem-solving is the cognitive process of identifying, analyzing, and resolving challenges or issues to reach well-considered solutions.

How it is used in consulting:

Now, girlfriend, in consulting you should expect that about once a week someone is going to ask you to do something you have never done before. What do you do? Probably your first instinct is to ask someone for help, but then you look around and you see everyone working on their own things. Then you think: "Well, they did hire me to do this job, I am qualified, and I will figure this out." Then off you go.

You are qualified and you just have to think it through. Here, your strategic and analytical skills come in handy. With your strategic skills you will be able to see what the long-term, high-level implications are, and with your analytical skills, you will be able to dissect the details and build the solution from the bottom up, based upon solid numbers.

Becoming a person who is able to sit with a problem, think about it, find the solution, and defend the solution is just so empowering. It makes you confident, and it really makes you believe in your own abilities and power. The better a problem-solver you become, the more likely you will receive new opportunities to help you advance and the stronger a candidate you will be if you ever decide to do something else.

If you don't know, now you know: A framework to problem-solve by McKinsey [27]:

1. **Defining the problem**: In consulting, it is important to understand that the apparent problem may not always be the actual problem. Similar to doctors, consultants should not solely rely on the initial diagnosis from the client. It is crucial to delve deeper, gather facts, ask probing questions, challenge assumptions, and uncover the true underlying problem.

2. **Identifying the root cause**: Instead of rushing to find a solution, it is essential to determine the root cause. Addressing only the symptoms may provide temporary relief, but the problem will persist unless the underlying cause is properly addressed and resolved.

3. **Employing a hypothesis-driven process**: To identify the root cause, consultants use

---

[27] Ethan M. Rasiel, *The McKinsey Way: Using the techniques of the world's top strategic consultants to help you and your business* (New York: McGraw-Hill, 1999).

an educated guess approach by formulating hypotheses (possible causes) such as A, B, and C. These hypotheses are then tested with data and facts, creating a process that is driven by evidence and analysis.

4. **Structuring the analysis with the "issue tree" framework**: Conducting a hypothesis-driven process can be time-consuming given the numerous possible root causes. Therefore, consultants employ an issue tree framework to break down and structure the analysis. This framework allows for a systematic exploration of hypotheses in a top-down manner, ensuring that the issue tree is mutually exclusive and collectively exhaustive (MECE).

5. **Proposing solutions**: Once the root causes have been identified through thorough analysis, you can propose targeted solutions that directly address these causes. By tackling the underlying issues, consultants can offer effective strategies to resolve the problem at its core.

6. **Present your thoughts**: Take your written thoughts and present them to your manager. For this step, you need assertiveness and confidence. Yes, the chance that people will do what YOU suggested is realistic, thought through, and possible. You should be so proud of that.

How is this skill useful in your future career:

Knowing that you can rely on yourself and that you will figure it out will save you so much stress in life. Since you know you will find a solution, there is no need to panic. And pushing through the insecurity creates resilience and inner strength.

Problem-solving is a critical skill that can greatly benefit your future career, regardless of the industry or profession you choose. Employers value individuals who can effectively identify challenges, analyze situations, and devise practical solutions. By honing your problem-solving abilities, you will become a valuable asset to any organization, making you a sought-after candidate for various roles.

In your future career, problem-solving will empower you to tackle complex tasks and overcome obstacles with confidence. For instance, if you are working in marketing, you may face the challenge of increasing brand awareness for a new product. Your problem-solving skills will enable you to conduct market research, identify target audiences, and develop creative strategies to reach potential customers effectively.

Similarly, in the field of technology, problem-solving will prove essential when troubleshooting technical issues or developing innovative solutions to enhance system efficiency. By analyzing data, identifying patterns, and collaborating with cross-functional teams, you will be able to implement successful changes that drive productivity and customer satisfaction.

Whether you are managing projects, leading teams, or contributing to innovative solutions, problem-solving will be your guiding force, propelling you toward success and recognition in your future career.

Building trust

#girlconsultant lifehacks:

"I learned you are nothing without a team. You are the team actually. So you should take care of them."—Igor, my prior boss

Collins English Dictionary describes trust this way: "If you trust someone, you believe that they are honest and sincere and will not deliberately do anything to harm you."[28] They say that trust can only be built over time, but it is also hard to build back after it has been broken. Trust is one of the main factors of a long-lasting relationship. And since this is a book about consulting, let's talk about work relationships.

At work, seldom will you always like and trust everyone you work with. With some people, you will have more banter and share deeper thoughts, with others you will not. And that is okay. You do not have to be best friends with everyone, but you can get along with each other and have a trusting work relationship. Now you may ask, "And how do I do that?" Well, I got you covered.

Charles H. Green created a formula for it. It is called the Trust Equation, and it focuses on "honesty, authenticity,

---

[28] "Definition of 'trust'", *Collins Dictionary*, 23.10.2024, https://www.collinsdictionary.com/dictionary/english/trust

paying attention to the other person, and being focused on the long-term relationship." [29] If you know this equation (which I've highlighted below) and have internalized it, it is easier for you to influence and set the tone in a relationship. Even when you have people who may not like you, or who may not want to trust you, by acting in specific ways, they have no choice but to at least say: "She is trustworthy." This is how powerful I think this equation is.

Here are some ways you might demonstrate you are trustworthy, according to the equation. You are knowledgeable about the topic you are working on. You reply to emails and return missed phone calls within 48 hours. You care about a person and are able to keep their secrets. Lastly, you really listen to others when they speak, and react accordingly. If you can demonstrate these things, you are on the perfect path for trustworthiness.

If you don't know, now you know:
The Trust Equation

$$\text{Trust} = \frac{(\text{Credibility} + \text{Reliability} + \text{Intimacy})}{\text{Self-Orientation}}$$

---

[29] David H. Maister, Robert M. Galford, and Charles H. Green, *The Trusted Advisor* (New York: Touchstone, 2001).

The trust equation provides a framework to understand the four elements that contribute to trustworthiness in professional relationships. It suggests that trust is built by combining three positive attributes (credibility [how believable you are], reliability [how dependable you are], and intimacy [how secure and comfortable others feel with you]) and then dividing by self-orientation (the degree to which a person is focused on their own interests rather than those of others). High levels of credibility, reliability, and intimacy, combined with a low level of self-orientation, result in greater trust.

Find details of this copyrighted process at trustedadvisor.com.

How it is used in your job in consulting:

Consulting is a people business. Essentially, what the client pays for is the consultant's brainpower. But how does the client know that you can solve her issue? She has to have trust in your partners' or company's ability to deliver. Thus, the partner had to build trust with the client, which is then the foundation of a long-lasting relationship. The ideal scenario is that both people are honest and have each other's best intentions at heart; however, sometimes in business this is not always possible. It may be that you really want to win the project and you, as a partner, believe you have the best solution to the client's problem. The client does not trust you though, because in general she has had a bad experience with consulting companies and is reluctant.

The Trust Equation is a little cheat sheet to support you in building trust with that client to secure the project and build a lasting relationship.

I know, I am speaking about partner-level engagement, but you can also do this on a more junior level. Say you are working with your client counterpart, and you need access to the numbers because you are supposed to calculate a business case. The counterpart does not want to give you the numbers, though, because she does not trust you. That is when you can take that person for coffee and get to know them on another level. Create a safe environment for them through empathy and little self-orientation, and you will improve the working relationship.

The Time I Did Not Pay Attention to Being Reliable, and Got the Boot

I could have done better. During my first projects in consulting, I had one boss who put a high emphasis on reliability. They even told me: "I am giving you small, easy tasks to see how you perform, so I can give you bigger tasks." Obviously, I did not listen, because I knew from experience that easy tasks bored me. I was too fabulous and smart for easy tasks. *flips hair*

As usual, I did not understand that this was a way for them to see if they could trust me. Well, needless to say, when the project ended, they gave me a bad review. Why? Because not only did I not do a good job, I did a poor job on the easy tasks, and then they gave me more and more easy tasks, which I did not do well, either. So, they never got to see how I would perform on the difficult tasks. Boom, a very low score in numerator (reliability), and the trust equation was off. Of course, I learned from my mistakes and now always give it my all, even on easy tasks.

How is this skill useful in your future career:

If there is one thing I learned, it is that we never just go to the office to do our work and then come home. At every workplace there is an ecosystem of different personalities, egos, issues, alliances, and politics that we sometimes have no idea about or no control over. To get ahead at work, you need to perform well, produce good work, and be considered trustworthy.

Trust is the foundation of strong professional relationships, and being able to establish and maintain trust with colleagues, clients, and superiors can open doors to new opportunities and advancements in your career. In a leadership role, building trust is essential for creating a cohesive and motivated team. When your team members trust your judgment and expertise, they are more likely to be engaged and committed to achieving shared goals. In client-facing roles, trust is paramount for winning and retaining business. Clients are more likely to work with individuals they trust, as they feel confident in your ability to deliver results and act in their best interest.

Building trust can also be beneficial in navigating workplace dynamics and managing conflicts. When colleagues trust your intentions and integrity, they are more likely to be open to resolving disagreements and working together toward mutually beneficial resolutions. Of course, it is very difficult to build trust with everyone you work with, but you should definitely pick out some key stakeholders and build trust intentionally. Maybe you actually genuinely like them and you want them to become your friend, or you just know they will be a key decision maker about where you go on your next project, so keep the trust equation in the back of your mind and use it to your advantage.

Networking

One skill worth learning in consulting is how to network. Networking is the art and practice of establishing and nurturing relationships with other individuals in both personal and professional contexts. It involves creating a web of connections that can lead to various opportunities, collaborations, and mutual support. Networking is not just about collecting business cards or adding contacts on social media platforms; it is about building authentic and meaningful relationships based on trust, respect, and shared interests. Networking is a valuable tool for career advancement, as it can lead to job referrals, mentorship, and access to hidden job markets.

If you don't know, now you know:

Networking is the art and practice of establishing and nurturing relationships with other individuals in both personal and professional contexts.

Networks are a long-term investment, and at the beginning, there is not much return. You might also feel put off when someone you do not know well or for long asks you for a favor. At least that is how I felt early on in my career. Having grown into the person that I am now, and after having invested into my network for ten years, I am slowly getting a return on my investment. I can ask for referrals. I can ask for introductions. And I can also ask for information from specialists in their fields. Because I have been in business for so long, I can also provide these kinds of services to my network. Networking is a long game but a game worth playing.

#girlconsultant lifehacks: Tips on How to Start Networking

1. Sign up for networking events in your area, including a women's network or even a career fair.

2. Develop an elevator pitch for yourself and practice it. Think about what you want to be known for and think of five stories that you can share about yourself.

3. Go to the event, stand straight, and smile.

4. Do not be afraid to introduce yourself to someone, but then also be brave and move on to meet other people, after a couple of minutes. You do not need to stick with the same person for the whole time.

5. Add everyone you meet on LinkedIn and write a short note on where you met, unless it is obvious because you work together.

If you don't know, now you know:

An elevator pitch is a brief, persuasive speech designed to spark interest and leave a memorable impression on the listener in the time it takes to ride an elevator, typically 30 seconds to two minutes. It serves as a concise and well-crafted introduction that succinctly conveys who you are, what you do, and what you have to offer. The goal of an elevator pitch is to capture the listener's attention, establish your credibility, and generate curiosity about your skills, products, or services. Whether used in networking events, job interviews, or business settings, an effective elevator pitch communicates your unique value proposition in a compelling manner, making it a valuable tool for personal branding and opening doors to new opportunities.

Different ways of networking

There are two different ways of networking. Neither is right or wrong. It just depends on what kind of person you are and what kind of person you want to be. There are advantages and disadvantages to both.

1. The Box Classifier

These are the people who collect contacts. They are the ones who will go to networking events, make the rounds with their elevator pitch, take the contact, and add them to LinkedIn. They are the ones who send LinkedIn requests without even knowing you.

Here, the relationship between these people is merely professional. It doesn't rely on trust. Box classifying can be used when meeting more senior people. A typical interaction is short and the questions that are asked are more like: "So what do you do?" and then you say what you do, so they know what you are good at. You can also ask them the same question to see if they are worth spending more time with because they are "useful" for your career.

Pros:

- In my experience, box classifiers would upload your resume on their company hiring portal and tell you about their job/company, but that is basically all they will do for you.

- A professional relationship can sometimes turn into a friendship.

Cons:

- Conversations are sometimes awkward, because both parties know it is just business.

- Since these relationships do not rely on trust, it is difficult to ask for favors or things that require effort.

- It requires a lot of effort to maintain the relationship, since the sheer amount of people to manage is substantial.

2. The Trust Builder

These are the people like a colleague I met in consulting, Luca, who builds trust intentionally. Trust builders ask good questions and have the people skills to ask in-depth questions without their counterpart getting scared. As humans, we do want to build a deeper connection with people, as that is what makes life and work enjoyable. I can recommend using this form of networking with your peers.

Pros:

- You are someone for sharing ideas, thoughts, resources, and stories with.
- You are helping someone and actually making an effort.
- You may actually become friends, which will last beyond that specific company.
- You may get quality recommendations, referrals, or introductions because they know, like, and trust you, and honestly want to help you out when you need one of these.
- They can share all the good gossip.

Cons:

- It takes time to have a conversation that will be remembered.
- It might be that when sharing stories with an aggressive or a passive-aggressive person, they can sometimes stab you in the back.

How it is used in your job in consulting:

In consulting specifically, networks are good for multiple things. First, inside the company, networking allows you to build a trusted circle of people who will support you and help you throughout your career. In my experience, people who are only looking out for their own benefit will not help you much in the long run. It might be a tit-for-tat kind of situation, but these people may switch sides quickly and may even spill your secrets.

Second, connecting with people outside of your company can help you get different views on an issue you might be having. This issue may refer to a business-related issue but can also be a people-related issue. Maybe you are being staffed on a project your colleague has been on, but she had a bad experience, which she would share with you so you can make an educated decision.

Third, networking and connecting with clients can help you with future job opportunities or future business opportunities for your consulting career.

How is this skill useful in your future career:

For centuries people have lived in groups, and the more curated and trustworthy your network is, the more benefit you will have from it in the long term. Motivational speaker Jim Rohn is often quoted as saying, "You are the average of the five people you spend the most time with."[30] If you start your career in consulting, you will meet smart people, and as you grow up together in the industry, you can support each other. A senior managing director once told me to find friends at work, because as we grow older and have more senior positions, we can help each other. In the future, you may also be able to help

---

[30] Mark John, "50 Jim Rohn Quotes on Success and Personal Development," The Inspiring Journal, May 10, 2015, https://www.theinspiringjournal. com/50-unforgettable-jim-rohn-quotes/.

each other with job opportunities and business advice, or you might end up starting a business together. Who knows? Curate the people who are around you; pick your friends and your acquaintances.

tl;dr

- Soft skills are crucial in consulting: communication, taking and asking for feedback, presentation skills, problem-solving, building relationships, and networking.

- Assertiveness and finding a balance between speaking and listening are important.

- Seek and provide feedback in a constructive manner.

- Develop strong presentation skills, including clear speaking, avoiding filler words, and using gestures effectively.

- Problem-solving is critical; embrace challenges, think critically, and propose well-reasoned solutions.

- Build relationships based on trust using the Trust Equation: credibility, reliability, intimacy, and low self-orientation.

- Networking is important for long-term career growth; consider different approaches like collecting contacts or building deeper connections.

- Stay authentic while adapting your communication style.

- Embrace continuous improvement and learn from feedback.

- Focus on continuous growth, reinvention, and becoming the person you want to be in your career.

PART 4:

BEING A WOMAN
IN CONSULTING

CHAPTER 11

Real Talk on Personal Branding, Company Politics, and Being Nice

W elcome to the last part of this book—part four. We'll be covering what I've learned about being a woman in consulting. Unfortunately, there are more men in consulting than women, which is one of the reasons I wrote this book: to motivate more women to join. In this first chapter of part four, I will tell you about the things that I learned the hard way, so that you do not have to—things like navigating company politics, developing your own personal brand, being nice (versus being assertive), and listening to your instincts. These are all as important as the other skills we discussed in the last couple of chapters. In fact, if we were to categorize these, we would call these "survival" skills. The hard and soft skills will help you thrive when you employ them the right way. What we talk about in this chapter will help you survive.

Company politics and personal branding

Maybe you see the word "politics" and you think: "Ugh, I hate politics." But the politics we are talking about are not the politics of a country or the world. We are talking about company politics. They are similar in a way, but also very different. Before we get into any definitions, let me explain why I think understanding company politics is important. The main reason is because when you play the political game right, you will have an easier time influencing the results you are looking for, such as getting the projects you want or landing the promotion you are after. Overall, you will have so much less frustration getting to where you want to go. So do not be like me, a person who had no clue about company politics until her 30s and who often did not get the things she wanted.

So, let's define what company politics are. Company politics refers to the intricate interactions and relationships within an organization. It encompasses the various ways in which individuals collaborate, form alliances, and make decisions to achieve common goals. These dynamics are influenced by personal and professional interests, differing objectives, and the allocation of limited resources. Effectively managing company politics involves understanding these interactions and using interpersonal skills and emotional intelligence to navigate the complexities of the workplace environment.

If you don't know, now you know:

Company politics refers to the intricate interactions and relationships within an organization. It encompasses the various ways in which individuals collaborate, form alliances, and make decisions to achieve common goals.

To do well in company politics, you need to set up your personal brand. Personal branding refers to developing a unique and distinctive identity, image, or reputation for yourself. It involves consciously and strategically showcasing one's skills, expertise, values, and personality to create a positive and memorable impression on others, especially in the professional sphere.

If you don't know, now you know:

Personal branding refers to developing a unique and distinctive identity, image, or reputation for yourself. It involves consciously and strategically showcasing one's skills, expertise, values, and personality to create a positive and memorable impression on others, especially in the professional sphere.

Personal branding is not only about self-promotion but also demonstrating authenticity, consistency, and expertise to build trust and meaningful connections with others. This means you have to start talking about yourself in the best possible way so that everyone knows your personal brand. I know we all grew up with the value of being humble, and I get that. Being humble is all about having a modest view of one's importance, achievements, and abilities. Humble people do not boast about their accomplishments, talents, or possessions. Instead, they display a down-to-earth attitude, acknowledging their limitations and being open to learning from others. However, when it comes to being humble, you have to pick your moments. These moments are usually with the people that you trust. With people in a position to choose you for something (a new project, opportunity, promotion, etc.), it is important to talk about your achievements in a way that aligns with your personal brand.

#girlconsultant lifehacks: A Quick How-to for Developing a Personal Brand

Step 1: Define the personal brand you want to be known for (e.g., smart, innovative, strategic thinker with industry specification).

Step 2: Think about the success stories that feed into this narrative. These stories may be still developing as you continue gaining experience, but you are looking for examples of your experience that support your brand. Look at projects you were (or are) staffed on and your achievements from those projects. For example, I was part of an innovation workshop for Dyson, and I came up with the idea for a new retail strategy. They are in the premium segment, and to reach more mainstream customers, I suggested they should have pop-up stores in high-end malls and give people blow-out hairstyles with their products, including a 10 percent off voucher for their immediate purchase. My strategy was considered innovative and valuable. This became one of my go-to success stories I could rely on when needed.

Step 3: When people ask you how things are going with your project portfolio, find ways to tell them the success stories you have defined in step 2.

Quick tips:

- You should have multiple stories that you can tell people about yourself and then use them when relevant to build your brand.

- Do not be shy about telling your stories to people you have just met. Be humble with the people you trust.

To counter unconscious bias, women should work on their personal brand

Most men in business obviously know other men, but because the number of women in consulting is so low, men tend to attribute the image that they have of a woman from their private life (their mother, sister, girlfriend, or spouse), onto the woman at work. This leads to a lot of unconscious biases which can impact you.

If you don't know, now you know:

Unconscious bias refers to the automatic and involuntary attitudes or stereotypes that individuals hold toward certain groups of people based on their background, characteristics, or other attributes.

The more women we have inside the workplace, and the more we bring our true selves to work and are not what people "expect" us to be, the more we can redefine the rules of the political game. Within the company I worked for, I knew exactly two managing directors who were women. One was a woman who climbed the ranks by (so I heard) keeping her head down, always working twice as much, and being three times better than her male colleagues. By being there long enough, people could not overlook her. She got promoted, because she was always the best. But she had to work twice as hard to prove it.

The other managing director was a woman who was a hoot outside of work, but at work, she was known as a badass boss. People were afraid of her. Everyone tiptoed around her. She climbed the ranks by behaving like a tough guy at work. She did not waste time on feel-good vibes and had a "tough love" approach instead. It seemed like I was the only one who was not afraid of her. I thought that her approach was cool. I thought not everyone had to be the same, and kudos to her for climbing the ranks like that. What I am trying to say is that back in the day, there were probably only these two approaches for a woman to make partners in consulting. Now, hopefully, we are further along and more women are promoted for being exactly who they are. Yet, regardless of who you are as a person, you need to have a strategy and a personal brand. Here is one example of how you can build your strategy in your company.

Sneaky Stakeholder Management

The company I was working for decided to launch a program called Reverse Mentoring, which essentially gave one person in their 20s the opportunity to sit in on all the managing directors' meetings and provide feedback on how to become more cool. I got picked to reverse-mentor the badass boss. I think I taught her some things, but she also taught me some things. Obviously, she was an expert in company politics, and although she wanted to revamp her branding amongst the younger people, she did know how to get a promotion. She shared her tactic with me, which now I want to share with you.

One key component to her strategy for promotion was that you had to be "visible." However, I just thought that meant people had to know and see you. I realized a little too late that in consulting, being visible means that people have to tell each other success stories about you. Something like: "Did you hear [name] did this? That is pretty awesome."

I presume everything people were saying about me was: "Did you see what she was wearing today? Did she also tell you that funny joke?" Clearly, I presented myself more as the fashionista or funny girl over the super brilliant and professional woman in consulting I now know I am. So, when it comes to being visible, make sure people are perceiving you the way you intend. From there, you can follow these steps (her steps) for rising through the ranks. Let's call the players Joana, the Managing Director, Level 3, who wanted to get promoted to Managing

Director, Level 2, and Kate, Managing Director, Level 1, the one who helped her.

- Step 1: Joana started by drawing a stakeholder map of people who were going to make the decision of her getting promoted.

- Step 2: Joana mapped out the influencers/ confidants of these decision-makers.

- Step 3: Joana mapped out who liked her and who did not.

- Step 4: Joana had Kate interact with the people who did not like Joana that much. Kate and Joana told a five-minute positive anecdote about Joana every time they spoke to someone on the stakeholder map and could influence the promotion decision. It takes at least five interactions to make someone change their mind about a person[31].

- Step 5: Tell the people that liked Joana more success stories about her and have regular interactions with them. Be "visible."

- Step 6: Lean back and watch how everyone talked well about Joana and watch how she got the things she wanted.

[31] Karen Munro, "At least seven touches: One academic library's marketing and outreach strategy for graduate professional programs," *Public Services Quarterly* 13, no. 3 (September 5, 2017): 200-206.

Joana got the promotion because first, she worked really hard and was successful and second, because she received support from Kate in building her personal brand and making it more positive. Both partners were deep in the political game, and they managed to change people's opinions of the partner through strategically telling success stories that aligned with Joana's personal brand and ultimately changed the result of the promotion decision in her favor.

Maybe right now you are thinking: "That's too much work!" I thought the same at the beginning of my work life and ended up making every mistake in the book. I always knew I had to be more strategic about my personal brand, but I just did not know how. No one gave me an approach until the day that partner shared her secrets.

Being nice even when facing unconscious bias

Remember, unconscious bias refers to the automatic and involuntary attitudes or stereotypes that individuals hold toward certain groups of people based on their background, characteristics, or other attributes. These biases are often deeply ingrained in our minds and can influence our perceptions, decisions, and actions without our conscious awareness. Unconscious bias can stem from societal influences, cultural conditioning, personal experiences, and media portrayal. It can manifest in various forms, such as gender bias, racial bias, age bias, and more. Despite being unintentional, unconscious biases can have significant consequences in various aspects of life, including the workplace, where they can impact hiring decisions, promotions, and interactions among colleagues.

During my first year in consulting, I noticed how unconscious biases toward women affected me:

1. **Comments about my appearance.** My seniors were trying to be nice, so they would point out things such as: "Your red nail color matches your red mouse." Or they would notice if I had been to the hairdresser. I know why; first they were trying to find a common ground with me, and because they had a wife and a daughter at home, this is what they thought they could talk to me about. *shaking my head*

2. **Administrative tasks delegated to me instead of more technical ones.** I was assigned to do most of the communication tasks and to build the relationships with the secretaries. Taking on communication for the project, going for lunch with the client team's secretary, booking the hotel rooms for the team, as well as reminding them to cancel when they were sick . . . which put me in the position of being a mom. Just because I am a woman does not mean I should have to do these things "because I am better at communicating."

3. **Assumptions about my skills based on gender stereotypes.** Because I speak several languages fluently, there was an assumption that I was not very good at Excel and numbers. This is the perception that either

you are good in languages or you are good in math, which is not true—you can be equally good in both. This bias was also stronger because people think girls are better at languages and boys are better at math.

Figuring Out How to Overcome Unconscious Bias

I started consulting when I was 23 years old. At the time, I thought if I wore a suit, I would look more "senior" and everyone would respect me, promote me, and think I was the real MVP (as in Most Valuable Player). I soon realized that there was more to being senior than just the look. Back then, I should have just accepted that I was in my early 20s and had to gain more experience. The seniority would come all by itself with time.

Instead, at the beginning, I was known as the #circusclown—the one who always cracked jokes—which did not help my seniority status. I thought, "Okay, how do I appear senior with the goal of getting promoted?" Having seen the guys who got promoted in my first year, I thought I needed to be tough like them. I thought the only way to succeed in the male-dominated business world was to be more like my male colleagues. *Really* male. Think, white boy "Chad": entitled, privileged, wearing a suit with loafers and pastel shirts, and smelling of arrogance. We have all seen them on TV, the Wall Street guys, the lawyers, or the high-profile consultants—all serious and too good for everyone else.

By the end of my first year, I took all my observations on unconscious bias into account and created a series of rules for me to follow. I knew I needed to switch strategies on how to get ahead. Humor was not making me the right connections. I thought I was not allowed to be too funny, too smiley, or too nice because it would undermine the respect and admiration I wanted from my co-workers. So here are the rules I decided to follow:

- I was not going to smile too much, I was going to be distant and reserved, hoping that then people would take me seriously and wait until I finished my sentence before interrupting me. How rude, I always thought, but it is work, so I could not be all *snap my fingers* and say: "Stop interrupting me, didn't your momma teach you some manners?"

- I was not going to be feminine in any kind of way, including being nice. Nice and kind are feminine traits. So I would not be nice or kind (or fun).

- I was going to be tough to earn respect. For me, at that time, the only way to appear tough was to go to work to do my work, only talk about work and then try not to show emotions and be mistaken as too "female."

Going into my second year, I made sure I did not laugh at too many jokes or smile too much, and I dressed in my pantsuits with my shirt buttoned all the way to the top. On one particular project, I decided I was going to be respected. So, I really tried hard to be a Chad. I was even wearing men's perfume.

As the weeks progressed, it was getting increasingly hard for me to play my "tough guy" role, and I began to think there should be another way to be tough without having to change one's whole personality.

Ruben joined me on the project. He was a good looking Spanish guy, three years younger than me. He only ever shaved on Sundays and when he came to work on Monday, because of his clean face and long eyelashes, he would soon be known as "Bambi." Bambi and I had the job of convincing one of the key users from the client's team to do things differently than he had done the past 20 years. This guy was a very difficult person. Everything he said was negative. He would complain about everything and he would find problems everywhere.

Bambi and I were on this project together with me trying to be tough, and him, well simply being himself. He was a nice guy. I had never seen him be entitled, mean, arrogant, or behave in any way like the typical Chad. This realization did not come immediately; I realized it over time. We were together in meetings with the client and our boss, and we worked on concepts, slides, and Excel sheets together. He was always precise in his answers, very calm and assertive with his communication, and never lost his temper. It must have taken me at least four months to realize this, but he was well respected by everyone on the project and by the client. And I could not help but wonder: "Can I be myself, be nice and be respected?"

The answer is yes, I just needed to know my boundaries and communicate them effectively, as we learned in the chapter on assertiveness. I needed to be confident in who I was and what I brought to the table. I needed to think about my personal branding and who I was allied with in the office. I could get ahead in my career if I paid attention to these things. Unconscious bias be damned.

Talking about boundaries, this leads me to the next topic:

Listen to your instincts and report harassment

Sexual harassment is a global issue. It is widely acknowledged that a significant number of sexual harassment cases go unreported. According to a US Equal Employment Opportunity Commission (EEOC) report, approximately 75 percent of people who experienced harassment at work did not report it.[32] The EEOC enforces federal laws prohibiting employment discrimination, including sexual harassment. In 2018 and 2021 the EEOC recovered $299.8 million for individuals with sexual harassment claims through resolved charge receipts and in litigation, benefiting 8,147 people.[33] Wow, right?

This topic is very close to my heart, because not only have I experienced it firsthand, but I think every woman should know that it is NOT okay for someone to force themselves on you at work without your consent. Then try and try again . . . . This. Is. Not. Normal.

I know what you are thinking at that moment. You might be worried that if you reject him or her, he or she will just keep bullying you at work. Or what if you tell someone and now that person starts treating you differently? Either way, please speak up. Do it for all the girls who come after you. If a

---

[32] U.S. Equal Employment Opportunity Commission, "Task Force Co-Chairs Call On Employers and Others to 'Reboot' Harassment Prevention," EEOC Newsroom, June 20, 2016, https://www.eeoc.gov/newsroom/task-force-co-chairs-call-employers-and-others-reboot-harassment-prevention.

[33] U.S. Equal Employment Opportunity Commission, "Sexual Harassment in Our Nation's Workplaces," EEOC Data Highlight, April 2022, https://www.eeoc.gov/data/sexual-harassment-our-nations-workplaces.

company does not have a speak-up culture, or treats you differently after something like this happens, then you should leave. Tell everyone about your experiences and leave. Even by sharing your story, you will have made an impact. The importance is always the impact. And once you close one door, another one opens. Trust me.

I'm going to share two stories with you. One when I was 25 years old, and really thought I sold my soul because I was too afraid to say something, and one when I was 30, when I had become more assertive.

Afraid to Speak Up

I received a call from my favorite boss, Igor. He told me I was to take over a project from a colleague. At the time, I had never heard of Igor. He was a manager from Spain. I had appeared on a random staffing list, got a call, an address, a time and date, and off I went.

The client was a manufacturing company in Germany. Except for a few HR ladies and some female secretaries, everyone else was male. The project lead on the client site, Mark, was a 30-something-year-old single guy. His boss, Steve, recently got married for the third time and was expecting a baby. He was in his 40s. He was also the head of the manufacturing plant. It seemed to me that the project was going to be more successful if we all spent more time together. We had a lot of meetings both in and outside of work. We had a small 15-minute meeting every morning, in addition to our two official jour-fixes every week. Even though we saw each other EVERY day, we also went out for dinner quite a bit to create good relationships.

Since I did not have a lot of experience on how close is too close while working with the client, I did not read anything into it when Steve tried to convince me that Mark's apartment was THE place to be, and I really had to see it as soon as possible. I did not see this as a sign. I was focused on the fact that the project was going well, Igor was impressed, and that I must be really smart for everything to be going so well.

When Igor flew in from Spain once a week, he came to dinner with us, but when he did not, if Mark and Steve invited me for dinner, I went. Mark was single, so he had nowhere to be after hours, and Steve's family lived three hours away; he stayed in a small apartment during the week, so he also had nowhere to be. We would also always work late, and maybe they felt guilty about keeping me there so long. My thought was, "Yay, free dinner!"

One evening after dinner, Steve had driven off to his apartment, and Mark pretended his car was parked very close to mine, because he wanted to make a move. While I was trying to say goodbye, he came closer and said: "I came to tell you that I have never met someone like you. I really like you. I want to spend more time with you, outside of work."

I froze. "Umm," was the only thing I could think to say followed by a long pause. Mark slowly came closer and kissed me. No tongue, thankfully. Just our lips pressed awkwardly against each other. Realizing what was happening, I pulled back and tried to find an excuse to get out of the situation.

"Okay, well, I'm tired and I still need to prepare something for our jour-fixe tomorrow." I quickly got in the car and sat there shaking for a few moments before I drove away.

Needless to say, THAT was awkward. And frankly, it was wrong. To put me in this position was selfish of Mark. I wanted to continue to do a great job at work. I had heard of so many stories of women rejecting advances and their lives would be made miserable. I was afraid the same might happen to me. So, I behaved like before, as if nothing had happened. I was still charming and went to all of his pretend meetings. I did not tell anyone about this. I felt embarrassed. I tried to laugh it off.

In the upcoming months that we worked together, he tried to tell me to stay at his place on the weekend, he wanted to invite me to a holiday, and he kept texting me nonstop. I was afraid I was going to be kicked off the project if I was not at least flirty and nice. So, I continued being nice.

In the end, it was a successful project. I still had not seen Mark's apartment, and I managed to maneuver the one-on-one meetings with Mark without any major issues. I rolled off the project and called it a day. I felt that I sold my soul by not saying something, and I should have been more assertive. I really should have been braver and told Mark, "Listen, I am not interested. If you continue this behavior, I have to speak up and report you to the compliance manager of my company." I should not have allowed that behavior.

When I Spoke Up

What I learned from my first story was that we have to be brave to speak up. If we want to make a difference, and create a better world, we have to speak up for the things that are not right, even if we take a beating or face a setback while doing it.

This next experience happened about five years after the first story. I really learned from my mistakes, and this time around I was brave enough to say something.

I was on a project for a big European company, and I was there to support some IT encryption team, to help them digitize. The project team on the customer side was around seven people, two of whom did IT support. The IT support guys were very geeky, and one of them, Matteo, did not speak to anyone else but me. Every time he saw me, he really made an effort to strike up a conversation about how my day was going.

Our offices were on opposite sides of the corridor. He would often leave his door open, so that whenever I walked to the kitchen to get some coffee, he could jump out of his chair and follow me. He would ask me if he could join me for a coffee, and my answer was usually, "For a quick one, yes"; after all, I was trying to be professional. I knew he liked me; he had been asking me for my private phone number. I kept saying no.

One day, he followed me into the kitchen, where he then stood in the doorway, looked me up and down, and said: "You know, I have." Knowing what he was going to say, I interrupted him:

"Yes, I know, I am fabulous; now get out of my way." Feeling greatly uncomfortable, I took my coffee and walked out the door, back to my office.

I thought this type of assertiveness and stronger language would make him back off. I had told him that I had a boyfriend and that I was not interested. Scenarios like this went on for a while, until the project was nearly finally coming to an end. There were only three more weeks to go.

Then one morning, Matteo was peeping out of his door checking if I had arrived to work yet. He arrived at the office around 7 a.m.; I arrived around 8:30 a.m. I usually went to my office, dropped off my stuff and was on the hunt for my second coffee, as I had drunk my first one at home. He asked me to come to his office; he said he had something to tell me. I put down my things and I made my way over.

He closed the door behind me. Then, he slowly came closer and grabbed my shoulders in an attempt to slowly push me against the wall. At first, I did not understand what was happening. I was touching the wall with my back, and his face came closer and closer, and I still did not get what was going on. The penny dropped when his lips were about to touch mine. He was actually leaning in for a kiss. I opened my eyes really wide and heard a clear "AHA," in my head. I pushed him away and asked for an explanation.

Obviously, I did not get one. He just murmured something like: "You drive me crazy," so I walked out of his office thinking, first of all, why did I not punch him, and second, who the hell does he think he is?

I walked back into my office and told my colleague what happened. He jumped up and asked if he should go punch him for me. I said no and sat down to breathe. Clearly, Matteo had no success asking me out during the whole project, so now he was trying one last time with force to make something happen before I left.

It was a whole commotion. The other team members, who saw me walk out of Matteo's office, came running. They asked me what was wrong, because my face looked all stressed and disgusted. So, I told them. One of them immediately reported the incident to his boss and told him that he did not want to work in such an environment. I felt very supported. His boss was the project leader on the client side, and he immediately took action. I then reported the incident to my boss, and I opened a ticket to internal investigations. Luckily everyone moved fast, and luckily Matteo was a subcontractor and was fired soon after. I had to go through some interviews explaining what exactly happened, which I did.

I decided that saying something right away was the right thing to do. It felt empowering and I felt supported. One thing that also changed was that I told this story to anyone who would listen. Even if internal investigations kept the information confidential, I was ready to tell people that these things still happen, and that we should watch out for each other. My goal was to empower other people to motivate victims of any form of harassment to speak up, because it is the only way we can change something.

tl;dr

- Recognize unconscious biases in the male-dominated workplace, but do not let them change you or doubt your capability.
- Master company politics and self-branding to build successful relationships.
- Be authentic and true to yourself; do not conform to traditional molds.
- Discover your version of "tough"—be determined and assertive without losing your personality.
- Speak up against inappropriate behavior to foster a respectful workplace.
- Value your time and contributions; communicate your successes.
- Embrace resilience and continuous improvement in your journey.
- Champion change for inclusivity and empowerment in the workplace.

CHAPTER 12

A Little Office Fashion "Deep Dive"

I love fashion, because I love the power of fashion. Fashion choices can influence how we perceive ourselves and how others perceive us. Dressing in a way that aligns with your personal style and values can enhance self-esteem and create a sense of empowerment. In this chapter, we explore the art of perception through fashion, delving into the unconscious decisions our brains make and the impact of clothing choices on our behavior and the behavior of others.

I will introduce a two-part framework, with the goal of enabling you to find your style while being in control of how you are perceived. The first part is on understanding the different outfit types, from basic to modern to extra, and what they suggest about the person wearing them. The second part is considering your outfit choice or style as it pertains to your boss' assertiveness type. For the purpose of this chapter and this conversation, I am focusing on the relationship between you and your boss, because it will be the relationship that has the most impact on your career. This framework is to give you full control of how you are perceived by making informed fashion decisions.

The connection between formal wear, assertiveness, and perception

Over the years there have been a multitude of studies conducted on the correlation between the impact of clothes on our own behavior and on the behavior of others. Formal clothes (such as suits, blazers, shirts, blouses, shift dresses, etc.) can make us take things less personally and make us feel more powerful and confident. In a study reported in 2014 in the Journal of Experimental Psychology: General, male subjects wore their usual streetwear and were then placed in either a suit or in sweats. [34] Then they engaged in a game that involved negotiating with a partner. Those who dressed in a suit obtained more profitable deals than the other two groups. This was largely because those who dressed up had higher testosterone levels than those who dressed down. This study found that formal clothes can have a psychological impact on both the performance of the wearer and the perceptions others have of us.

Let me tell you about another study, a very old one.[35] This study's findings, presented at the meeting of the American Psychological Association in 1967, were based on an experiment manipulating social settings to explore the impact on other people's self-image and confidence. In the experiment,

[34] Michael W. Kraus and Wendy Berry Mendes, "Sartorial symbols of social class elicit class-consistent behavioral and physiological responses: a dyadic approach," *Journal of Experimental Psychology: General* 143, no. 6 (2014): 2330, https://psycnet.apa.org/record/2014-38364-001.
[35] Stanley J. Morse and Kenneth J. Gergen, "Social Comparison, Self-Consistency and the Presentation of Self," *American Psychological Association* (September 1967), https://files.eric.ed.gov/fulltext/ED019680.pdf.

researchers tried to explore how the presence of contrasting individuals impacted the self-image and confidence of others. Specifically, they created two distinct personas and presented them to a group of undergraduate men going for an interview: A "Mr. Clean" (well-dressed, groomed, and self-assured), and a "Mr. Dirty" (embodying contrasting traits), and measured self-esteem and situational perception of the group of men. These personas altered the self-esteem of the undergraduate men. The authors found that regardless of the competitive or non-competitive nature of the situation, the presence of an individual with socially desirable characteristics (like Mr. Clean) led to a decrease in the self-esteem of the undergraduate men, while an individual with negative characteristics (like Mr. Dirty) caused an increase in the undergraduate mens' self-esteem. What does this study teach us? It teaches us that in every situation, most of us probably compare ourselves with others. We define if our self-esteem is above or below the person who is in front of us. If it is below, we usually try to lift ourselves up and present our achievements, showcase our expensive watches, brands, cars, and may also even lie to close the gap toward our counterpart. On the other hand, if our status is higher than our counterparts, we may react by trying to make ourselves and our achievements small and brush them off to make the other person feel better. According to my experience, if you want to be the real MVP, your feelings of self-confidence and assertiveness stay constant no matter who is in front of you. This may throw people off, but in the end, this is how you can stay authentic, content, and free.

If you don't know, now you know: Ways That Formal Attire May Influence Assertiveness

Perception: Dressing in formal attire can influence how others perceive you in a professional setting. It may convey a sense of competence, credibility, and authority, which can positively impact how others interact with you and respond to your assertiveness.

Mindset and confidence: Dressing formally can create a mental shift, signaling that it's time to adopt a more serious and professional mindset. This shift can boost confidence and help you feel more empowered to express your opinions, needs, and boundaries assertively.

Social norms: In many workplace environments, formal attire aligns with social norms and expectations. Conforming to these norms can foster a sense of belonging and help you navigate the professional environment more effectively. It can also enhance your confidence in communicating assertively within those established norms.

Another study, "The Cognitive Consequences of Formal Clothing" in 2015,[36] analyzed how formal attire can change people's thought processes. "Putting on formal clothes makes us feel powerful, and that changes the basic way we see the world," says Abraham Rutchick, an author of the study and a professor of psychology at California State University, Northridge. Rutchick and his co-authors found that wearing clothing that is more formal than usual makes people think more broadly and holistically, rather than narrowly, and about fine-grained details. The study also found that when wearing a suit, critical feedback was taken less personally, with less impact on people's self-esteem. This effect also does not wear off (no pun intended), no matter how often you wear the clothes. Interestingly, wearing a suit encourages people to use abstract processing, rather than concrete processing. Concrete processing is valuable for tasks that require practical implementation and direct understanding, while abstract processing is essential for grasping complex concepts, making connections between ideas, and developing broader insights. In consulting, you will be advising management on concepts, insights, and strategies, where abstract thinking is needed. Formal attire can help you manage this task more easily.

The halo effect, cognitive bias, and fashion statements

No one ever sees a person's personality in the first two minutes. Every superficial visual characteristic helps to put people into

---

[36] Michael L. Slepian, Simon N. Ferber, Joshua M. Gold, and Abraham M. Rutchick, "The Cognitive Consequences of Formal Clothing," *Social Psychological and Personality Science* 6, no. 6 (2015): 661-668, https://www.columbia.edu/~ms4992/Publications/2015_Slepian-Ferber-Gold-Rutchick_Clothing-Formality_SPPS.pdf.

categories: the way they carry themselves, the way they dress, the way they walk. Depending on these superficial things, we deduce if a person is smart, rich, powerful, important, etc. This is the cognitive bias called the "halo effect."[37] It occurs when our overall impression of a person is influenced by our initial positive perception of them in one specific area, leading us to assume they possess other positive qualities as well, even if there is no evidence to support those assumptions.

If you don't know, now you know:

The halo effect is a cognitive bias that influences how we perceive and judge others based on a single positive trait or characteristic.

Since the 1920s, this bias has been examined in multiple studies. A study conducted by Landy and Sigall demonstrated the impact of the halo effect when males made judgments on female academic competence, and attractive women were evaluated as more competent.[38] A research study conducted in

[37] R. E. Nisbett and T. D. Wilson, "The halo effect: Evidence for unconscious alteration of judgments," *Journal of Personality and Social Psychology* 35, no. 4 (1977): 250–256, https://doi.org/10.1037/0022-3514.35.4.250.

[38] David Landy and Harold Sigall, "Beauty is talent: Task evaluation as a function of the performer's physical attractiveness," *Journal of Personality and Social Psychology* 29, no. 3 (1974): 299.

1968 by Rosenthal and Jacobson discovered that teachers generally develop expectations for their students based not merely on the school record but also on their physical appearance.[39] In the areas of people, company, brand, and product, the outcomes have been similar throughout the years. For example, if someone is physically attractive, we may automatically assume they are also intelligent, kind, and competent, without any direct evidence of these qualities. This bias can work in various domains, including physical appearance, social skills, or professional achievements.

The halo effect can have both positive and negative consequences. On the positive side, it can lead to more favorable judgments and opportunities for those who possess certain positive traits. However, it can also lead to inaccurate assessments and biased decision-making, as we may overlook or downplay negative traits or behaviors that do not align with our initial positive perception.

It is important to be aware of the halo effect and to make a conscious effort to evaluate individuals based on a comprehensive assessment of their qualities, skills, and actions rather than relying solely on initial impressions or single positive traits. This helps to promote fair and unbiased judgments and avoid making assumptions based on limited information.

The halo effect speaks about the benefits someone has when they are attractive, and attractiveness does not necessarily mean physical attractiveness (like being a model). Attractiveness refers to the subjective perception of qualities or features

---

[39] Margaret M. Clifford and Elaine Walster, "The effect of physical attractiveness on teacher expectations," *Sociology of Education* 46, no. 2 (Spring 1973): 248-258, https://www.jstor.org/stable/2112099.

in a person that evoke positive feelings, admiration, and a desire for engagement or connection. It encompasses both physical attributes, such as appearance and body language, as well as intangible qualities like personality, confidence, and charisma. Factors that influence your attractiveness or appearance are your clothes and your level of grooming. You can be any shape, color, or size, but as long as you look put together, you will appear attractive. You don't believe me? Just look at all the makeover shows, such as *Queer Eye*; they always focus on internal and external factors. Grooming and wardrobe are a main factor in how someone feels about themselves and how others perceive them in return. I am trying to tell you that with the right wardrobe, you are already halfway to making use of the halo effect.

The Time I Confirmed the Halo Effect

I stood in the office kitchen wanting to get a coffee, when my colleague came around the corner at the same time. She also wanted to get a coffee—the usual after-lunch productivity dip. We hugged and started chatting. She had also been with the company for two years at that point and was starting to look around for other options to check her market value. "Interesting," I said, "and you just apply to random consulting companies and see what kind of job you would get?" She nodded. She continued to tell me about her recent applications.

I liked her strategy, so I started applying. "I haven't been to Hamburg in a while, maybe I should apply to any consultancy and then get a free plane ticket," I thought.

Two weeks later I was sitting on the plane still contemplating whether I made the right outfit choice. I was going to do my own little experiment to test the effect clothing had in an interview. I wanted to test the limits of the halo effect. I was curious to see if people would have an underlying bias toward me as a woman, assuming we are not analytical enough. I was also 25 at the time, and by the looks of this old picture I probably did not come across as very senior. Confident, yes, but not senior. Seniority, for me, definitely came with age.

I had chosen super-chic gray high heels, a gray dress with an A-line skirt, and a dark gray cardigan. So yes, 50 shades of gray.

Fast forward to the interview, and of course, I had to do an estimation case. So, I am cracking the case. It is a very small boutique company, and everyone is very polite. After the interview, I spent my afternoon visiting friends before I headed back to the airport. As I flew back, I could not help but wonder: "Would they make me an offer for the highly analytical position I had applied for, even though I was dressed in a flowy, non-structured, feminine way?"

I hypothesized they would not make me an offer and would say that I was not structured enough. I am usually very structured in my thoughts, so the causality of the halo effect would go as follows (mind you all this clustering is done in the first two minutes and it is done unconsciously):

- Here is a young woman, well groomed, yet feminine-looking.

- She is smiling and polite, so she must be a good communicator, and it is probably fun to go for coffee with her.

- She is wearing a flowy dress and a cardigan without structure; thus, she must not be good at structuring things.

- Gray is a boring color; she must not be very interesting as a person.

- Would I like to work with her? Probably not. She is more like a nice wallflower and it would be difficult to work with her, because it would be hard for her to follow the train of thought.

I waited a week to hear back from them, and then I got the email that I did not get an offer. I was curious to know why, so I called, because people do not like to give reasons via email.

The voice on the other side said: "We did not take you because we thought you were not analytical and structured enough."

There we go! Case in point. Hypothesis confirmed. I had a very methodical and structured approach and cracked the case, yet I believe that they undervalued me because of how they perceived me. I was also probably not confident and senior enough to pull off this outfit. More on that later.

What makes an outfit interesting and gives the right impression

You may ask: So #girlconsultant, what should I wear to work then that is not boring and also gives the right impression? I do not want to wear a boring black or dark blue suit, with a white blouse. It is just not me. I am also not going to a funeral.

I then would answer: Your outfit does not need to be boring. With the right accessories and the right combinations, it will look just like you. It will be interesting and fabulous.

I get it—it also never used to be me. I spent my school years in a hoodie, jeans, and a T-shirt. My mom would force me to wear a blouse when we went to our grandma's. She would always say: "Can you for once just look a little bit more elegant?" I hated it, but also because the blouses I had were ill-fitting, low thread count, and stiff. So, girl, I know the trauma, but let me change your mind. First, however, I would like to explain what an interesting outfit is.

An outfit is interesting if the eye can wander. This means that the eye will find different points to look at, moving around the outfit, from the socks to the collar to the rings on your fingers. Keep it tasteful though; do not overload it and look like a lit Christmas tree.

For example: if you are wearing a blue suit, a white shirt, and just orange socks, the eye will directly go to the socks. But if you pair your orange socks with orange cufflinks or an orange pocket square, the eye can wander from the socks to the cufflinks to the pocket square.

Unlike other style guides, I have tried to stay away from rules, because honestly, that stuff is so outdated. If you do not know what I am referring to, I mean things like: you should ALWAYS wear tights, even in the hottest of all summers. Your skirts should never be too short; one palm length over the knee is the shortest you should go. Your heels are not supposed to be too high, and plateau stilettos are forbidden. You catch my drift?

Take these "rules" and throw them out of the window. Especially after the pandemic, they are not relevant anymore. However, I want to make you aware that fashion holds a lot of power that you should be aware of, and in the end, it is your decision. As mentioned in the chapter intro, I have created a two-part framework for this, and here is the first part.

Dress for success framework
PART 1: Before anything, consider your confidence and seniority

I have put together some standard ways of dressing that are common for the consulting industry. But as with everything, *it always depends,* and for this part of the framework, depending on how confident you are as a person and how senior you are, you would dress differently. Hear me out:

Confidence: Confidence comes from inside. I can best describe it as: imagine you are wearing a bright pink feather boa, with a sparkly dress, and you are talking to a judge. If you are 100 percent confident, you focus so much on the content of the conversation that you totally forget how you are dressed and how others may perceive you. You would not apologize for being dressed like that or make up a story that you came from a birthday party and did not have time to change. You would just walk in, shoulders back, look the judge straight in the eye, and make your case. Now, this is a very extreme example, but I hope you get the idea. Translating this into the business world, if you have that kind of confidence, you can wear anything and everything and probably be taken seriously.

Seniority: From what I have observed, especially in the workplace, when people do not know you, they assume things. They assume things according to how you dress, because that is the easiest way to judge and our brains are lazy, so they categorize you into a box with a label, and then they look to confirm that label with everything you do.

When you start off in a company, of course, you want to stand out and make a name for yourself, but then you need to define for yourself: under what label do you want people to remember you? The easiest way to label yourself as professional, hard-working, smart, and determined, especially in consulting, is to dress in more muted colors and a suit. Taking this thought logically to the next step would mean that once people know you, and the label in their minds is attached to the adjectives mentioned before, you can start relaxing or changing your dress style. Because now, no one will question your ability if you wear big hoop earrings or funky loafers to work. It is just your style, and it has nothing to do with your competence.

I used to have a rule that on every project I worked on, I would exclusively wear pantsuits and a white blouse for two weeks straight to brand myself as smart, attentive, and professional. After the two weeks, I would then relax my style, and wear more dresses and skirts and more turtlenecks. It always worked like a charm. As they say, there is no second chance to make a first impression.

#girlconsultant lifehacks: Style Considerations for Creating a Successful Image in Consulting

Still unsure of what to wear? Do not stress! Your fashionista personal assistant is here! (That is me!) Read the next section for all the styles you can consider creating for a successful image in consulting.

The Classic Basic Outfit

Wear this if you want to be on the safe side in consulting. You can dress this look up and down, by taking off the blazer and rolling up the sleeves, if you feel that the current situation calls for it or if it is hot in summer. You can also wear different suit styles (e.g. oversized, double breasted blazer, long flared pants, high waisted pants, or over the ankle pants).

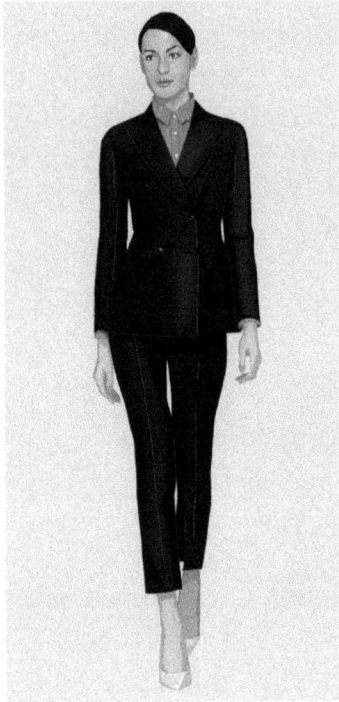

Here are examples of what you can wear:

- Color palette: Blue, white, brown, black, green, shades of grey
- Type of suit: Navy blue suit, dark green suit
- Type of top: White/light blue blouse/ turtleneck

- Type of accessory: Black or brown belt
- Type of shoes: Black or brown shoes (high heels or flats, should be leather or vegan leather)

Go to girlconsultant.com for more inspiration.

The Modern Consulting Outfit

Depending on what industry you work in, pairing a suit with a pair of sneakers can make you look dynamic and modern. People who work in digitization and IT are especially likely to wear this kind of outfit, because if you want to be at the forefront of technology, you cannot rock up in an outfit that reminds you of the '50s.

Here are examples of what you can wear:

- Color palette: All shades of blue, white, beige, brown, black, green, gray, or a bright color (e.g., red/orange)

- Type of suit: Blue/gray/green suit with pants/skirt/dress with a different texture, or pattern. Broken suit (different colored jacket and pants)

- Type of top: Colorful blouse/jumper/turtleneck/top

- Type of belts: Belt that fits in any color, really

- Type of shoes: Flats or high heels, sneakers (preferably without pattern. All white sneakers really look the best)

Go to girlconsultant.com for more inspiration.

The Extra Consultant Outfit

Once you have a reputation as a smart, successful woman who has a lot of experience, you can basically wear what you like. This is what I was referring to with having enough confidence, and seniority. You can go all feminine, or all dandy, or all jewelry, or all colorful. And honestly, you should, pushing the boundaries of what it means to be a woman in the workplace. You can be assertive and charismatic, be an engineer, and wear a yellow flowy skirt and an orange blazer. In a perfect world, this should not have any impact on how capable people think you are, but according to my observations, there is still a lot of work to do before we get to that point.

The only thing here is I would say to just try and look like you. Put effort into the outfit, so the clothes should be clean and ironed, and maybe no holes. I have also worn my Zara jumpers with a hole on the sleeve to client lunches by mistake, and it did not really hurt me, so you do you—just be mindful.

Here are some examples of what you can wear:

- **Color palette**: Here really any color is fine; just remember that darker colors add gravitas to an outfit, and light, colorful ones animate.

- **Type of suit**: If you wear a suit, a jumper (sweater), and a skirt, or a dress, with or without a blazer, anything goes. You can also wear jeans or smart shorts in summer. Just try not to look like you are going to the beach.

- **Type of top**: Jumper, turtleneck, large knit jumper in winter, and tops for summer. Maybe not spaghetti strap tops, but if it is really hot in summer, then go for it.

- **Type of belts**: Wear whatever belt you like: with glitz and gold, with silver lettering; go for it.

- **Type of shoes**: In western Europe, open toe shoes like wedges are not really seen that often, due to the generally colder weather. In southern Europe, such as Spain or Portugal, due to the extreme heat in summer, most people wear open shoes to work. When it comes to this one, knock yourself out with any other shoe option that you like.

Go to girlconsultant.com for more inspiration.

PART 2: Fashion is Power—How to Dress Depending on Your Boss' Level of Assertiveness

Now that I have told you all about fashion and the different outfit types, let me tell you about how to combine this with your boss' assertiveness type. You may ask "why do I need to adapt and why do I need to be the bigger person? Why can the other person not adapt to me?" Because if you adapt and are the bigger person, you are actually the one in control, regardless of your title or theirs. And if you are in control, you have the power to influence the other person to think the things you want them to think.

Being assertive means taking matters into your own hands, communicating effectively, and leading the conversation to where you want it to go. I do not mean to overwhelm you into thinking that every conversation you have needs to be calculated and outcome-driven. However, I do know from experience that there will always be certain crucial meetings or conversations at work where it pays off to think about what you want out of it, even if it is just an honest answer to a question. In these moments, it is vital to step into your power and use it. Lead the conversation, be the bigger person, be assertive and outcome-driven. The following framework can help with this.

The assertiveness fashion framework

With a little help from my dear friend and psychologist, Dr. Bianca Serwinski, we came up with an assertive fashion framework where we match the consulting outfit styles (mentioned previously) to the kind of person your boss is. I hope you will work together with lots of assertive people, but in case you don't, here is a guide on how to manage situations that may emerge from the way you dress.

When dressing for an occasion or a person, it is not about fulfilling someone's expectations—it is about putting yourself in the position of power. You get to decide how other people see you and thus what they will think of you. This framework will help you decide what to wear, depending on the level of assertiveness of the person in front of you.

Since you know that the way to always be professional and successful is to be assertive, in this framework, we are assuming that you are assertive, or at least on a good path to becoming your best assertive self.

Scenario 1: You are assertive, your counterpart is passive

When dealing with a passive counterpart, it is important to consider dressing in a way that promotes a comfortable and approachable atmosphere. Here are some pointers on what you could wear:

Casual and relaxed: Opt for a more casual and relaxed attire that can help create a comfortable environment. This can include clothing such as a clean and well-fitted shirt or blouse, paired with casual pants or a skirt. Avoid overly formal or intimidating clothing choices that may create unnecessary tension.

Soft colors and patterns: Choose clothing in soft colors or subtle patterns that can create a calming and non-threatening ambiance. Light pastels or earth tones can help foster a relaxed atmosphere and put the passive individual at ease.

Friendly and approachable: Dress in a way that reflects a friendly and approachable demeanor. Consider incorporating elements such as a smile, maintaining good eye contact, and using open body language to create a welcoming atmosphere.

Comfortable fabrics: Opt for clothing made from comfortable fabrics that allow for ease of movement. This can help convey a sense of ease and relaxation, which may help the passive individual feel more comfortable in your presence.

Your outfit of choice should be: The Modern Consulting Outfit!

Scenario 2: You are assertive, your counterpart is passive-aggressive

When interacting with a passive-aggressive counterpart, it's important to prioritize your own comfort and confidence while maintaining professionalism. Here are some general tips for dressing in such situations:

Professional and polished: Opt for professional attire that aligns with the expectations of your workplace or the specific setting. Choose clothing that is well-fitted, neat, and in good condition. This can help you project a sense of competence and professionalism.

Neutral colors: Wearing neutral colors, such as black, gray, navy, or beige, can help maintain a calm and composed appearance. These colors are generally less likely to draw attention or evoke strong reactions, allowing the focus to remain on the conversation or work at hand.

Comfortable yet confident: Choose clothing that makes you feel comfortable and at ease, while also exuding confidence. When you feel good in what you are wearing, it can positively impact your mindset and help you navigate challenging situations with more ease.

Approachable, but assertive: Aim for an approachable yet assertive appearance. This can include a friendly demeanor, good posture, and maintaining eye contact. Dressing in a way that reflects your personal style, within the boundaries of professionalism, can help you feel more authentic and self-assured.

Your outfit of choice should be: The Classic Basic Outfit!

Scenario 3: You are assertive, your counterpart is aggressive

When dealing with an aggressive counterpart, it is important to prioritize your own safety, comfort, and confidence while maintaining professionalism. Here are some things to consider when dealing with an aggressive person.

Professional and assertive: Dress in a professional and polished manner to project a sense of confidence and competence. Choose attire that aligns with the expectations of your workplace or the specific setting. Opt for well-fitted clothing in good condition that gives you a professional appearance.

Neutral and non-confrontational colors: Choose neutral colors that are less likely to evoke strong reactions, such as black, gray, navy, or beige. These colors can help maintain a calm and composed appearance, avoiding unnecessary distractions or confrontations based on clothing choices.

Comfortable and empowering: Select clothing that makes you feel comfortable, empowered, and ready to handle challenging situations. When you feel confident and at ease in what you are wearing, it can positively impact your mindset and help you navigate aggressive encounters with more composure.

Your outfit of choice should be: The Classic Basic Outfit!

Scenario 4: You are assertive, your counterpart is assertive

If both you and I are assertive, it is important to dress in a manner that reflects confidence, professionalism, and personal style. Basically, you can wear whatever you like. Here is a suggestion on what you could be looking for:

Assertive yet approachable: Choose clothing that balances assertiveness with approachability. Opt for attire that exudes confidence while still maintaining a friendly and welcoming demeanor.

Strong colors and patterns: Consider incorporating bold colors or patterns that make a statement and showcase your assertiveness. Choose colors that suit your complexion and complement your personal style, whether that is vibrant hues or sophisticated patterns.

Statement accessories: Add statement accessories that enhance your outfit and highlight your assertive personality. This could include a bold watch, a statement necklace, or a power tie. Choose accessories that align with your personal style and enhance your overall appearance.

Your outfit of choice should be: The Extra Consultant Outfit!

The Woman in the Red Dress and
The Power of Fashion

It was International Women's Day, 2015. We were all invited to celebrate the day in the HQ of the company. Just before the big speech, we mingled and had coffee, when a woman in a red dress appeared on the scene. She walked in, had a coffee, and left. I was curious who she was and what she was doing here. I was too timid to ask her back then, but I would soon find out anyway.

As we sat in the big auditorium, guess who walked in? The lady with the red dress. She was a profiler. A profiler is an individual who analyzes behavior, characteristics, and evidence to create a profile of a person, typically for the purpose of criminal investigations. They use psychological and investigative techniques to identify patterns, motives, and potential suspects based on the available information.

It seemed like she knew something I did not, so I listened up. She gave a speech about work and perception, and first of all, she also spoke about her red dress. How we must all be categorizing her, probably thinking that she does not belong in a business setting. How we may be thinking that she may be using her looks and way of dressing to get attention. She mentioned that we are all guilty of judging books by the cover, and that she picked out this red dress to make exactly that statement. She wanted to show us, women and men, how we all have that unconscious bias.

We have unconscious biases, predominantly rooted in culture and the way we were brought up. With this story, I want to make you aware of this particular clothing bias (along with many other biases that exist) and to be careful about its impact when it is important, where impressions matter and can influence your career progression.

tl;dr

- Fashion has the power to boost confidence, shape perceptions, and enhance self-esteem and empowerment.

- Formal attire can positively influence how others perceive you in professional settings, conveying competence, credibility, and authority.

- Dressing formally can create a mental shift, boosting confidence and enabling individuals to express their opinions and needs assertively.

- Conforming to social norms of attire in the workplace can foster a sense of belonging and help navigate the professional environment effectively.

- The halo effect influences how we judge others based on initial positive perceptions, highlighting the importance of comprehensive assessments and avoiding assumptions based on limited information.

- Fashion can be used for self-branding and creating a successful image in different professional contexts.

- The framework explores outfit styles, based on confidence and seniority, and how to adapt dressing based on counterparts' levels of assertiveness to influence perceptions and outcomes.

CHAPTER 13

When #girlconsultants Travel

I n this chapter, we will explore practical travel hacks designed specifically for women in the consulting industry. Business travel can be challenging, but with the right strategies, you can make your journeys more comfortable and convenient while maintaining a healthy work-life balance. This chapter will provide valuable insights and tips to help you navigate the world of business travel like a pro.

Consultants and frequent flyers

Consulting and traveling are synonymous. Maybe you knew this, but in case you did not, here is a quick elaboration of a consultant's travel schedule: Usually, when you are staffed on a project (you know what that is from chapter 7), you would travel to the client site to be close to them, so that communication paths are short. Depending on the company you work for, you as a #girlconsultant would either book your flights, trains, and hotels via the company travel tool or via the travel agency that books everything for you. Monday early morning you would select a mode of transportation of your preference that does not take forever (either by plane, car, or train), and make your way to the client's site. You would stay overnight in a hotel and on Thursday make your way back home around 5 p.m. On Fridays, consultants usually go to their company's office to meet with colleagues and connect with people that are not staffed on the same project. However, since the pandemic, and since the movement toward avoiding unnecessary CO_2 emissions, companies aim to staff locally (the client HQ is in or near the same town in which the consultants live) and keep the travel to a minimum.

Below are some of my travel hacks that I have accumulated over the years and that you need to know:

Efficient travel planning:

Get in on the deets:

Whenever you travel, you need to be in specific places at specific times. Knowing what airport or train station is the closest, most frequented, or easiest to get to is important. On every project, there should be a way to learn how to get to the client's office. Check with your manager or colleagues to learn if there is a car service, a rental service, or a project car. Also check if there is a designated hotel chain where your project team will stay. Check the weather beforehand, if you are flying to a different country, and check the local customs and transportation options. Lastly, check the time you should be at your client's office for that first day, so that you can get the flight required. Try to keep the paperwork on your phone as much as possible. Save the address of where you need to go and get the tickets and apps on your phone, so that you have everything together. Even if your phone's battery runs out, you would still have your laptop to charge it with, and in case you lose it, make sure you have everything backed up in the cloud.

Point by point until diamond status:

When you travel a lot, you have the opportunity to get in on the loyalty programs of the big hotels and airlines. Usually the project has a dedicated project hotel, which is probably one of the big chains, and you already have a company discount there. The big chains come with a status and point system, which you can then also use for your private travels.

I remember I got upgraded to Diamond status on my third project because my manager had convinced the hotel manager to give all of the project members that status. It was really fun being able to take the first flight from Düsseldorf, Germany, to Vienna, Austria, check into the hotel at 9 a.m., go to the members' lounge, and have a big breakfast before heading to the client's office to start my work week. I would also like to add that making nice with the hotel receptionist does not really have much of an effect on your stay unless you have an elite travel status. Then, they can give you a good upgrade if you ask them nicely.

To lounge or not to lounge?

The same point system also goes for airlines—the more you fly, the more points you get, and then you get access to the airport lounges. Usually, every airport has one or two lounges, and if you have enough points with one airline, you can access a lounge. Sometimes the big airlines have their own members' lounges and are part of the OneWorld loyalty program, which allows you access to the OneWorld lounge in other airports. Usually in the lounge you have a buffet with sandwiches, some cooked food, and a variety of alcoholic and non-alcoholic drinks.

Now, there are two types of people: the ones who will go to the airport three hours in advance to sit in the lounge and enjoy the free food and drinks, or people like me. I always came last minute to the airport, just when boarding started, and then hurried to my plane, with maybe a minute to buy a bottle of water at a duty-free shop. This is a personal preference, so here you are on your own. A travel status does help frequent flyers avoid long lines at security, and you have more luggage allowance if you are like me and always arrive late.

Contingency planning:

There may always be some things you cannot predict: too much traffic on the way to the airport, too many people in front of you at security, a train breakdown, or being pulled over for speeding on the motorway. Who knows! The only thing I can say is if you are late, ask the airport staff for help to let you pass the line. If the airport staff says no, which they do in Zürich airport, then girlfriend, you just need to push past everyone. I have done it a couple of times. It works quite well; you just need to be alone and in a real hurry.

If your flights are delayed, there are ways to get your money back, but depending on where you are in the world, the regulations might be different. Do not panic though. Meetings can also be done remotely—sometimes that is just the best way to go.

Travel safety tips:

This depends where you are in the world; however, one thing I can always recommend is to keep your things with you. Close the zipper of your bag, take the official taxis from the airport, and lock your hotel room at night. A colleague once got robbed in Frankfurt, Germany, in his hotel room during the night because his door did not close properly and he did not notice it was not closed. This is shocking, but things like this can happen. You do not have to be paranoid or afraid, just be aware of your surroundings. The same goes for your hotel key card. Do not leave it in the envelope with your room number and name. This is dangerous if you go clubbing and you lose your card, or someone steals it. They can then go to your hotel and ask for a spare key and also come and rob you during the night.

Document management:

Have your passport/ID always in a safe place when you travel. If you take it out of your bag in the hotel, put it in the safe or in your locked suitcase. Please do not put it in a drawer of the nightstand and then leave it there. Also always carry around a digital copy with you, in case you do lose it or forget it.

Packing Tips

Suitcase choices:

I could go on and on about this topic . . . my attitude on suitcases is "the cheaper the better." I am all for a hardcover, as they call it, but there are two types of hard covers. One is very hard and can break easily if it is too full and then it gets tossed around. (It has happened to me with an expensive bag after three months). Then there is the not-so-hard one, also called a "soft shell," which is my favorite. You can still sit on it to close the suitcase; it is light and can be tossed around due to its flexible build. The third option is one of fabric; they usually come with an extra compartment for the laptop, but it takes a lot of space away from the inside. I don't like this model, as I always pack to the rim and keep my laptop in my work bag. I actually had a suitcase from a discounter for five years, and the only thing that was getting worse were the wheels. Otherwise, it was perfect. See my recommendation on brands and useability on girlconsultant.com.

Packing cubes and organizers:

Packing cubes and organizers are bag-in-bag systems—small-or medium-sized pouches where you can put your socks, tights, panties, and bras and have a bag just for dirty laundry. Your cosmetics, hair things, and your jewelry should also be in a separate bag or case. These tools will help you maximize space and keep belongings organized.

Travel-sized toiletries:

I mean, we all know about this, but just as a reminder, take your own shampoo and conditioner; the ones in the hotels usually are not good for you. Take your creams, deodorants, hairspray, nail varnish remover, hair oil, and body lotion (this list is non-exhaustive) in small containers. Also, if you do not have an airline status yet and do not have special fast treatment, checking your luggage may take time—time you could use to get home earlier on a Thursday evening.

Clear nail varnish:

Take one small bottle of clear nail varnish with you, in case those tights rip. You know what I mean. I have had so many situations where either I had holes in the toes, or around the waistband, and when this happens it just helps to be prepared. You can go to the bathroom quickly and put some nail varnish on the hole in the tights to avoid a long tear.

Hair dryer:

Take your own good hair dryer. I know how sacred all our hair is to us girls, and I can tell you that the ones in the hotels usually damage your hair, because they have no heat control built in.

Tiny handbag:

Take a little tiny handbag for dinner where you can put your wallet, phones, and room key. Usually, before we went for dinner, we went to drop our things off at the hotel. Then I just took my wallet, my two phones (one work, one personal) and my hotel key with me. Since women's clothing does not always have pockets, I carried everything around in my hands. Then, I lost my room key somewhere, so eventually I started taking a small bag with me so it would not happen again.

#girlconsultant lifehack: A packing list for your suitcase for a four-day trip

Have a list of things you need for your travels somewhere (maybe on your phone) so that when you pack your suitcase, you do not have to start from scratch but can easily make sure you have everything for the four-day work week. Here was mine:

- Clothes:
    - 7 pairs of underwear (it is always good to have spares, in case your plans change)
    - 5 pairs of socks
    - 2 pairs of tights
    - 2 bras (one beige, one black)
    - 4 tops (to wear underneath the shirts or jumpers)
    - 2 jumpers (in winter); 2 tops (in summer)
    - 2 white blouses
    - 1 pantsuit (that I would wear on the flight)
    - 1 skirt (in case I wanted to switch it up)
    - 1 pair of high heels
    - 1 pair of flats
    - Pajamas
    - Hoodie (for winter)
    - Small bag (for phone, wallet, and keys)
    - Optional: Sport things (in case you have time and energy for a workout)
    - Optional: Swimsuit (in case your hotel has a pool)

- Hair and Beauty:
  - Hairdryer
  - Brush
  - Hair oil
  - Makeup: foundation, mascara, bronzer, lipstick
  - Makeup remover + pads
  - Toothbrush and toothpaste
  - Shower gel, shampoo, conditioner
  - Creams and lotions
  - Jewelry
  - Nail varnish + nail varnish remover pads
- Food
- Medicine
- Electronics:
  - Laptop
  - Phone
  - Earphones
  - Chargers and cables
  - All other gadgets
- Money and credit cards
- Optional: Small hand steamer/straightening iron (the latter in case you want straighten your hair or iron the collar of your shirt)

Business travel attire:

Don't pack too much:

Stay with the basics—do not be like my old teacher, who chaperoned our senior year trip to Barcelona, Spain. We went for five days, I think, and she took two humongous suitcases with her because every day she would wear a different outfit, matching from head to toe. I can only suggest that you take what you need and then wear that. That is the beauty of the outfits we discussed in chapter 12. Wearing a suit is so easy to pack for, and so easy to wear, because you are always dressed, no matter where you go.

Capsule collections:

There are also very good capsule collections, where every piece goes with every other piece. You would then have a minimal amount of clothes and so many combination possibilities, so that you will never get bored with any outfit. Check to find good capsule collection examples on girlconsultant.com.

Fabric Choices:

Wrinkle-free fabrics ARE A MUST (at least for blouses). For every other piece stick to natural fabrics. Except: avoid linen, including in summer, because within the first minute—I am not kidding—of wearing anything in linen, the wrinkles start to show. Take cotton or silk fabric for shirts; they will keep you cool in summer and warm in winter. For dresses, try viscose as a fabric choice; it is very comfortable and does not wrinkle. Take a small steamer or a straightening iron if you need your clothes to be extra wrinkle-free.

Bag choices:

Get a good bag with a zipper, a latch to fix it on your trolley, a good organizing system inside, a comfortable length of the bag straps, and a cute color. Now you may wonder where to find such a bag at a good price point—and let me tell you I was looking everywhere for it and could not find it anywhere. The options that were available were certainly not affordable, so I designed and got them produced myself. I called it The Interstella workbag. While this fabulous bag is not currently on the market (at the time of this writing), it was the direct result of knowing what I needed for traveling as a #girlconsultant. So, even though you cannot purchase this exact bag at the moment, be on the lookout for a bag that has a main zipper, plenty of storage, and organizational compartments. When you find it, get it! It will be worth your investment. (The other option, of course, is to follow me so if I ever bring The Interstella Workbag back (more in chapter 14), you will be the first to know.)

Shoe choices:

This is a very personal thing, depending on how relevant comfort is for you. I used to wear my heels everywhere, to the airport, on the flight, at the restaurant, because I was all about keeping up appearances. I still really love high heels, but nowadays, I value comfort more than I used to. So now I would always pick sneaker outfits for travel days. Try what works best for you, but one thing I can say is: if you take high heels, also take a flat option with you.

Winter extras:

In winter, take thick pajamas; you never know how the heating will be in the hotels you will stay at. And the worst is getting sick because you were cold at night. Once I was in a hotel in the middle of nowhere in winter, and the cold air entered through the crack in the windows. The blanket was really light, and the heater did not really heat much. I complained and changed rooms, but that did not help. So next week I rocked up with long pajamas, a hoodie, and a pair of joggers. I was not getting sick because I was cold at night.

tl;dr

- Check the weather, use hotel and airline loyalty programs, and practice contingency planning for more efficient travel planning.
- Pack efficiently using packing cubes, organizers, and separate bags for specific items to help maximize space and keep belongings organized.

- Bring travel-sized toiletries, a small bottle of nail varnish, and your own hair dryer to enhance your travel experience.

- Simplify the packing process by creating a packing list and sticking to basics in business travel attire.

- Choose wrinkle-free and natural fabrics for clothing, invest in a quality bag, and consider capsule collections to help create versatile and stylish outfits while traveling.

CHAPTER 14

When #girlconsultants Are Badass and Have Work-Work Balance

Being in consulting taught me that everything is possible. I got to push the boundaries of what I thought I was capable of. In consulting, I was constantly confronted with tasks which I had no idea how to do, and with research, diligence, and determination, I always managed to figure it out. Pair that with the fact that I am a millennial, and we are known for trying to make our hobbies into our side hustle. So, that is what I did, using everything I had come to learn from consulting.

My hobby had always been fashion, because I was fascinated with how a good outfit could impact my mood and my performance. So, I started my own fashion brand, Corner Office, focusing on made-to-measure blouses and super chic, practical work handbags, such as the Interstella I mentioned in chapter 13.

Why I started Corner Office:

I definitely had some pain points I wanted to fix. I must have been three years into consulting when I got fed up with the fact that the men on my team always had really nice suits with nice thick shirts that fit, and that had a button row that could be closed to the top. After three years of wearing three different shades of blue suits and a lot of shift dresses, I decided it would be cool to start wearing something more edgy.

My dream was to have a tartan suit, and to wear my shirts buttoned up to the top. It was a vibe. I found a tartan wool suit for winter, but I was missing the shirt.

I mean, at work, we girls have to worry about working, and then we also have to worry about whether when we show someone something on the screen they can see down our blouse (or between the buttons). I was fed up with having to consciously think about so many things that my male colleagues didn't have to think about, so I decided to do something about it.

When I started:

It took me a long time to actually start, because I kept telling myself: "This weekend, I will sit down for two hours and work on Corner Office." For the first six months, that did not happen, because I always found an excuse of why I should start the next weekend. But then I thought, why not do a little bit every day, and after a while I will have a whole lot to look back on. So that is what I did.

Each day from the cab, the bus, or the train, I wrote to suppliers, created content for my Instagram page, or wrote a story for my blog, #thegirlconsultant, about things I had experienced and things that I wish I had done differently. I remember going for dinner with my colleagues, and while waiting for the food, I was on my phone sending emails to suppliers, or doing something to move forward with my brand. I mean, I was allowed to type away on my phone. I was with my colleagues the whole day, there was no obligation to ALSO talk to them during dinner. They had each other, so it was not awkward or anything.

How it went:

Nothing ever really goes as planned, including starting a business. First, I collected all the information that I needed to start a fashion business. I was set on the theory, or so I thought: Step 1: Create designs. Step 2: Find a production company. Step 3: Produce samples. Step 4: Get the garments made. Step 5: Sell. Now it was time to put that into practice.

I found a designer who knew what she was doing, and she did the designs for me. I loved every single piece that she made. Next was looking for a production facility with a low minimum order (meaning I would not have to order that many at a time, thereby reducing initial costs by not having to buy in huge bulk amounts). The first complication was that I could not find a decently priced production company that had low minimums which included the patterns. I thought if the patterns are the obstacle, let me pay someone to get the patterns and samples made. I got the samples made, but then I was asking myself, how many pieces will I get made in which sizes? Then I thought, why not go on Kickstarter (a crowdfunding platform where creators can pitch projects to a global audience to get financial support) and try and get some funding?

Kickstarter is a lot of work. Preparing the campaign content, creating the marketing materials, motivating people to buy something that they might not like without proper return policies, and designing and ordering the packaging. I used all my overtime hours to take two months off my consulting work to do all the prep work for Corner Office.

Next, I went live with the campaign, and I sent it to a lot of people including people at work, as they were women in business; they were my target group. Someone forwarded it to HR and I got a warning from work and had to shut down my campaign. Well, no risk, no fun, I would say. Honestly, I was not going to make my target funding goal anyway, and I also did not want to invest my own money to make it look like I made the goal and then pay a bunch of fees to Kickstarter.

As per Kickstarter policy, no one got anything. Tough luck. But I did not let that stop me. I got up, dusted myself off and decided to find another way. (Obviously, before dusting myself off, I cried for a week over what a failure I was, but I guess that is the journey of an entrepreneur.)

I thought it was best to get to know my customer. It was important to validate if their pain points were my pain points, too. I decided to focus on made-to-measure blouses, because I would have a lot of time with my customers. (You know, who were also my colleagues.)

After having successfully launched my made-to-measure business, my friend Ksenia (who also worked many years in consulting) came and said we should do practical, chic, #girlconsultant travel bags. And that is exactly what we did. We created the first batch. People could choose the type of leather and color, and we sold out. Then, the pandemic hit the world and no one needed any work and travel bags anymore, because they were not going to work anymore. Eventually I decided to put all my Corner Office products on hold because no one knew how the post-pandemic world was going to look. So, in the meantime I focused on other things (like writing this book).

What I learned from a business perspective:

Corner Office was my self-taught and guided MBA. In other words, I did not return to school for the graduate-level degree program that provides students with comprehensive knowledge and skills in various aspects of business management, including finance, marketing, operations, and entrepreneurship. I did not read a lot of case studies of situations that may or may not have happened inside a classroom setting. What I did do was gain real-life experience.

I learned that although I calculated a business case before diving into this whole endeavor, in the end I was really far from the budget because things came up that were impossible to assume at the beginning, such as marketing costs. I had no idea that photographers, videographers, ads, and props were so expensive. I always asked my friends to model for me, but I paid for everyone else.

The next thing I learned was that Porter's Five Forces is right. I was a little delusional at the beginning, and I did NOT do a Porter's Five Forces analysis, because I was sure I knew about the fashion industry. For example, the threat of substitute products is high for women, because we have so many options when it comes to wearing something. To work, we can wear a blouse, a top, a turtleneck, a jumper, a dress, a cardigan, long sleeves, short sleeves, etc. In the end, my customers only bought one good made-to-measure blouse. I had expected that the time I invested in the beginning—to take the measurements, to pick the cut and the fabric—would lead to more consecutive sales, but they did not, so my business case was wrong again.

As you can see, there was a lot of learning, but probably the biggest learning was that sales and business development are the most important thing for a small business. As a one-woman show (the founder, the CEO, the accountant, the creative, and the product designer), it is difficult to do any sales. In my next business, I will definitely hire a salesperson, because it is always easier to talk about someone else's achievements than one's own.

What I learned from a personal perspective:

I definitely improved my networking and sales skills by wearing the products and showing them off. The hardest part about this was when I knew someone and then felt personally rejected if they did not like the garment. What also stressed me was sending something to a customer and then never getting feedback. Did they actually wear the garment, and did it make them feel empowered when wearing it? As a result of both of these, I learned how to handle both not receiving any feedback and getting bad feedback. I would have to remind myself that this was business, not personal.

I also had to leverage my problem-solving skills a lot. Speaking to my customers let me understand their pain points, what they were looking for, and how I could make their life easier. For example, I incorporated a small push button (a snap) between the buttons around the boobs, so that there was no way someone could sneak a peek while wearing a Corner Office blouse. I also had to solve problems within the company. How would I design the packaging now that I had different measurements for the Interstella work bags and the blouses? How do I send anything abroad? How do I get more clients outside of networking? All these are questions that I had to think about, research, and solve.

In consulting, I was thrown into the deep end and had to swim over and over again. Sometimes I swam, but sometimes I needed someone to throw me a buoy. This made me nurture my resilience, which made me realize and understand that whatever I put my mind to, I can achieve. If I needed help, I would look for the right person and pay for their services. Even though Corner Office in its first form was not the typical definition of "success," at least I learned a lot. I pushed my boundaries and believed in myself. It is hard to believe in yourself, as we sometimes have people around us that don't believe in us. So, the only one who is always clapping and cheering us on needs to be us. But I would not have had the gumption or self-confidence or even skill set to give this a try had it not been for everything I learned in consulting. Consulting is like a gateway to endless possibility.

tl;dr

- If you really want to do something on the side, you will find time no matter what.

- Small steps every day amount to so much over time.

- Consulting experience will minimize your fear of starting a small business or pursuing any other hobby, because you will know that as you go along, you will figure it out.

- Consulting also teaches you self-confidence and that you need to be your own cheerleader.

- Explore new things. Learning is never a lost effort or investment; it always means new skills learned.

- Grow resilient and find different approaches if things do not work out.

- Use all the skills from consulting to help navigate the challenges of any side hustle or new endeavor.

Conclusion

Girlfriend, you made it. You have reached the end of this book. I think you and I have become besties. You know me better than most people, and I hope to hear from you about your journey, too, so join the community on social: @girlconsultant. As you may remember, my goal was to give you an honest review of consulting as a career choice and to empower your decision of whether to go into consulting. Of course, I hope you will feel empowered to give consulting a try; otherwise, I would not have shared all my secrets with you. But ultimately, the choice is yours. The question at the beginning was: To consult, or not to consult. Remember? I am excited to know what your verdict is.

In this book, I took you through the basics of what you need to know about the consulting industry, then we moved on to interviewing and getting hired and how to set yourself up for success. I shared with you my assertiveness framework, the hard and soft skills you will need, ways to personally brand and network, and even how to dress for success. I offered you my best tips, tricks, and hacks through these pages so you can be a successful woman in consulting.

Out of all the things you have read, here are some things I would especially like you to walk away with:

1. Be authentic and show up confidently.
2. Really work on your assertiveness, because that is a skill that will be useful no matter what.

3. Dress according to the situation, if you like to think about the details of fashion. If not, always pick the suit—you can never go wrong.

4. Recognize that when you learn skills in one place, they can transfer into other places in your career.

5. Speak up and do not compromise your values; leave the company and move on.

6. Work hard, but do not lose yourself.

7. Make friends, but do not trust everyone.

We evolve through all our experiences and any time we try anything new: Growth takes us out of our comfort zone, and we should grow; otherwise, life becomes monotonous. I was once in your shoes and I did not know anything about consulting, and now I am writing a book about it—and just through the process of writing the book, I learned a lot about myself. I have gotten out of my comfort zone, and I am putting my successes, my struggles, and my opinions out there. I wrote this book while working a full-time job. It required a lot of discipline and self-motivation. Writing about all the consulting topics has made me realize what a great playground consulting was. I have not gone back to consulting yet, but I am also not ruling it out for the future. So, stay tuned!

I hope you had a fabulous time reading this book, I hope you learned from my mistakes, and I hope you will be one heck of a #girlconsultant. If you do not have a cheerleader, or someone who believes in you, then remember that you will always have me. You are fierce, strong, resilient, and capable. Always remember that even when things are hard, or challenges surmount, you are not failing, you are growing. Keep taking small steps every day, and you will have come a long way over time. You've got this!

Ta ta for now, dahling . . .

xo,
Your #girlconsultant mentor and guide,
Tanja

Afterword

I embarked on my consulting journey over a decade ago, and as you've seen throughout this book, I haven't just high-lighted my triumphs but also the challenges I've conquered. These experiences have been invaluable, shaping me into the successful professional I am today. Consulting has been an extraordinary teacher, and I want to share one more story that encapsulates my journey.

Recently I took a flight to London for a weekend getaway with my friend Bianca—a classic girls' weekend. The plane was small, with just one aisle and two rows of seats on either side. I settled into my seat, opened my laptop, and made sure I had everything ready to work for the flight. Out of the corner of my eye, I noticed the guy sitting next to me scrolling through what looked like my LinkedIn profile. He must have seen my email or username from my laptop and decided to look me up. He got stuck at my consulting experience. I found it cheeky but flattering, and I continued working, knowing my profile must have made quite an impression

Around one hour into the flight, he struck up a conversation about how they only serve water on the flight and I was thinking, well, he clearly doesn't fly with this airline often, so no wonder he is confused. I politely ended the conversation to focus on my work. He also worked for a while until he pulled out an old-school leather organizer, and I caught a glimpse of a business card with the name of the consulting company I used to work for. I was curious but focused on getting through my tasks, so I didn't say anything right away. However, when we landed, I couldn't resist asking, "So, do you also work for (insert name of my former employer)?"

He looked up and, with a hint of surprise, replied, "Yes."

I told him I noticed him checking out my LinkedIn profile, and though he felt a bit embarrassed, I assured him I do the same sometimes. That broke the ice, and we started chatting. He shared that he was a Managing Director at said consulting company and had been with them for 27 years. We discussed our mutual connections, my #girlconsultant journey, and our experiences in the industry.

Our conversation eventually touched on the topic of sexual harassment, this time from the perspective of someone in a senior position. He mentioned that he often brings a chaperone to events and after-work gatherings to have a witness in case of any false accusations. He explained that some people harbor resentment, possibly believing he was responsible for them not being promoted, and might act on revenge fantasies. This was an eye-opener for me and something I felt compelled to share. My takeaway from this story is a hope that no one is ever wrongfully accused, just as much as I hope no one ever denies responsibility for their actions. This unexpected encounter also opened new doors for me in promoting this book and gaining insights into the ever-changing consulting industry.

Since my consulting days, I've worked for multiple Fortune 500 companies, excelling in roles ranging from innovations manager, to logistics country manager, to sales professional. My diverse skill set, honed through years of high-stakes consulting, has made me a sought-after profes-sional, frequently headhunted by industry leaders. These for-mative years trained me to spot opportunities, allowing me to build an ever-growing network of professionals across the globe who continue to rise through the ranks. With every-thing I've mastered—the soft skills, the hard skills, the asser-tiveness, and the seniority—I decided to dive headfirst into entrepreneurship with full confidence. And this time, I'm not just diving—I'm swimming laps around the pool. I'm now a full-time entrepreneur with a thriving business that's grow-ing exponentially. The world is my oyster, and consulting was the launchpad for my success, truly tying everything together. What I can do, you can do too, dear #girlconsultant. Now go get 'em!

About the Author

Tanja Deisler, MIB, began her career at a leading American consulting firm in Germany. Being one of the few women in manufacturing and engineering consulting, she has gained unique insights that spurred both personal and professional growth. Her keen sense of observation and reflection led her to write this book to offer the guidance and advice she wished she had before she started her consulting career. She is a successful business professional and entrepreneur. Tanja is also the founder of #girlconsultant, a company that extends the book's practical wisdom to support aspiring consultants, particularly women. Her efforts focus on empowerment through mentorship and resources, making her a pivotal figure in the consulting industry.

For more info visit: girlconsultant.com

Acknowledgements

I want to express my deepest gratitude to everyone who has believed in me. Your unwavering support has always meant the world to me.

Special thanks goes to my amazing partner, David, thank you for your endless love, patience, and encouragement. Your belief in me that I can do anything, is my greatest strength.

Thank you to Ally, my incredible book coach. Your brilliance, structure, and creativity guided me through the writing process, and I couldn't have done it without you.

My heartfelt thanks to my best friend, Bianca Serwinski, for co-writing the assertiveness chapter with me and for always being my cheerleader. Your support has been invaluable.

I am immensely grateful to my beta readers for their time and detailed feedback: Dina H., Manja K., Murat B., Ruben G., Silvia G., Sinead R., Usman R., Verena S., Warren L-N., and, of course, my mum. Your insights helped shape this book into what it is today.

Thank you to the incredibly talented Kim Raaf, the best photographer I know and a dear friend. Thank you for capturing the cover image so beautifully. Your talent and friendship mean so much to me. I love watching your adventures and high-profile weddings around the world.

Lastly, I want to thank my brilliant publisher, PYP, for making this book a reality. Your expertise and dedication were instrumental in bringing my vision to life.

And a big shout-out to Gilberto P. for, well, doing absolutely nothing, but for still wanting to be part of this journey. Your humor never fails to bring a smile to my face.

References

Adler, Ronald B., Lawrence B. Rosenfeld, and Russell F. Proctor. *Interplay: The Process of Interpersonal Communication.* 14th ed., Oxford University Press, 2018. 77.

Aragão, Carolina. "Gender pay gap in US hasn't changed much in two decades." Pew Research Center. March 1, 2023. https://www.pewresearch.org/short-reads/2023/03/01/gender-pay-gap-facts/.

Bogdanich, Walt, and Michael Forsythe. *When McKinsey Comes to Town: The Hidden Influence of the World's Most Powerful Consulting Firm.* New York: Doubleday, 2022.

Boyles, Michael. "What is business strategy & why is it important?" *Harvard Business School Online – Business Insights,* October 20, 2022, https://online.hbs.edu/blog/post/what-is-business-strategy.

Bridgman, Todd, Stephen Cummings, and John Ballard. "What the Case Study Method Really Teaches." *Harvard Business Review,* December 2021. https://hbr.org/2021/12/what-the-case-study-method-really-teaches.

Clifford, Margaret M., and Elaine Walster. "The effect of physical attractiveness on teacher expectations." *Sociology of Education* 46, no. 2 (Spring 1973). https://www.jstor.org/stable/2112099.

"Definition of 'trust'", *Collins Dictionary*, https://www.collinsdictionary.com/dictionary/english/trust

"Definition of 'passive'", *Collins Dictionary*, https://www.collinsdictionary.com/dictionary/english/passive

"Definition of 'assertive'", *Collins Dictionary*, https://www.collinsdictionary.com/dictionary/english/assertive

"Definition of 'passive-aggressive'", *Collins Dictionary*, https://www.collinsdictionary.com/dictionary/english/passive-aggressive

"Definition of 'aggressive'", *Collins Dictionary*, https://www.collinsdictionary.com/dictionary/english/aggressive

"Definition of 'trust'", *Collins Dictionary*, https://www.collinsdictionary.com/dictionary/english/trust

Greiner, L. E., and R.O. Metzger. *Consulting to Management*. Englewood Cliffs, NJ: Prentice-Hall, 1983.

Grohol, John M., PsyD. "What's the Purpose of the Fight or Flight Response?" World of Psychology Blog. December 4, 2012. Archived at https://web.archive.org/web/20130323170934/ http://psychcentral.com/blog/archives/2012/12/04/whats-the-purpose-of-the-fight-or-flight-response/.

Herrity, Jennifer. "What Does It Mean To Be Professional?" Indeed.com. March 11, 2023. https://www.indeed.com/career-advice/career-development/what-does-it-mean-to-be-professional.

Ihenyen, Confidence Joel, PhD, Michael Ayakoroma,, and Emomoemi Egiye. "Transparency, Accountability, and

Investment Decision-making: the Case of Enron and Arthur Anderson." *EPRA International Journal of Economics, Business and Management Studies (EBMS)* 10, no. 9 (September 2023).

Jay, E. "Do the rich and famous really work harder?" *The Literary Review* 39, no. 3, (1996).

John, Mark. "50 Jim Rohn Quotes on Success and Personal Development." The Inspiring Journal. May 10, 2015. https://www.theinspiringjournal.com/50-unforgettable-jim-rohn-quotes/.

Kraus, Michael W., and Wendy Berry Mendes. "Sartorial symbols of social class elicit class-consistent behavioral and physiological responses: a dyadic approach." *Journal of Experimental Psychology: General* 143, no. 6 (2014). https://psycnet.apa.org/record/2014-38364-001.

Landy, David and Harold Sigall. "Beauty is talent: Task evaluation as a function of the performer's physical attractiveness." *Journal of Personality and Social Psychology* 29, no. 3 (1974).

Lorr, Maurice and William W. More. "Four dimensions of assertiveness." *Multivariate Behavioral Research* 15, no. 2 (1980).

Maister, David H., Robert M. Galford, and Charles H. Green. *The Trusted Advisor*. New York: Touchstone, 2001.

"Management Consulting." Consultancy.org. Accessed July 10, 2024. https://www.consultancy.org/consulting-industry/management-consulting.

Morse, Stanley J., and Kenneth J. Gergen. "Social Comparison, Self-Consistency and the Presentation of Self." *American*

Psychological Association 16 (September 1967). https://files.eric.ed.gov/fulltext/ED019680.pdf.

Munro, Karea. "At least seven touches: One academic library's marketing and outreach strategy for graduate professional programs." *Public Services Quarterly* 13, no. 3 (2017).

My Consulting Coach. "Case Interview Preparation." Accessed August 24, 2024. https://www.myconsultingcoach.com/case-interview.

Nisbett, R. E., and T. D. Wilson. "The halo effect: Evidence for unconscious alteration of judgments." *Journal of Personality and Social Psychology* 35, no. 4 (1977). https://doi.org/10.1037/0022-3514.35.4.250.

Porter, Michael E. "The Five Competitive Forces that Shape Strategy." *Harvard Business Review* 86 (2008).

Rasiel, Ethan M. *The McKinsey Way: Using the techniques of the world's top strategic consultants to help you and your business.* New York: McGraw-Hill, 1999.

Sandberg, Sheryl, and Nell Scovell. *Lean In: Women, Work, and the Will to Lead.* New York: Knopf Doubleday Publishing Group, 2013.

Schmidt, Günter, and Wilbert Wilhelm. "Strategic, Tactical and Operational Decisions in Multi-national Logistics Networks: A Review and Discussion of Modeling Issues." *International Journal of Production Research* 38, no. 7 (May 2000). https://doi.org/10.1080/002075400188690.

Schneiderman, Neil, Gail Ironson, and Scott D. Siegel. "Stress and health: psychological, behavioral, and biological determinants." *Annual Review of Clinical Psychology*, no. 1, (2005). https://www.ncbi.nlm.nih.gov/pmc/articles/PMC2568977/.

Slepian, Michael L., Simon N. Ferber, Joshua M. Gold, and Abraham M. Rutchick. "The Cognitive Consequences of Formal Clothing." *Social Psychological and Personality Science* 6, no. 6 (2015). https://www.columbia.edu/~ms4992/Publications/2015_Slepian-Ferber-Gold-Rutchick_Clothing-Formality_SPPS.pdf.28.

Statista. "Consulting services industry worldwide - statistics & facts." Statista. March 21, 2024. Accessed May 26, 2024. https://www.statista.com/topics/8112/global-consulting-services-industry/#topicOverview.

Tutor2u. "Biopsychology: The 'Fight or Flight' Response – Evaluation." March 22, 2021. https://www.tutor2u.net/psychology/reference/biopsychology-the-fight-or-flight response-evaluation.

U.S. Equal Employment Opportunity Commission. "Task Force Co-Chairs Call On Employers and Others to 'Reboot' Harassment Prevention." EEOC Newsroom. June 20, 2016. https://www.eeoc.gov/newsroom/task-force-co-chairs-call-employers-and-others-reboot-harassment-prevention.

U.S. Equal Employment Opportunity Commission. "Sexual Harassment in Our Nation's Workplaces." EEOC Data Highlight. April 2022. https://www.eeoc.gov/data/sexual-harassment-our-nations-workplaces.

The B Corp Movement

Certified

Corporation

Dear reader,

Thank you for reading this book and joining the Publish Your Purpose community! You are joining a special group of people who aim to make the world a better place.

What's Publish Your Purpose About?

Our mission is to elevate the voices often excluded from traditional publishing. We intentionally seek out authors and storytellers with diverse backgrounds, life experiences, and unique perspectives to publish books that will make an impact in the world.

Beyond our books, we are focused on tangible, action-based change. As a woman- and LGBTQ+-owned company, we are committed to reducing inequality, lowering levels of poverty, creating a healthier environment, building stronger communities, and creating high-quality jobs with dignity and purpose.

As a Certified B Corporation, we use business as a force for good. We join a community of mission-driven companies building a more equitable, inclusive, and sustainable global economy. B Corporations must meet high standards of transparency, social and environmental performance, and accountability as determined by the nonprofit B Lab. The certification process is rigorous and ongoing (with a recertification requirement every three years).

How Do We Do This?

We intentionally partner with socially and economically disadvantaged businesses that meet our sustainability goals. We embrace and encourage our authors and employee's differences in race, age, color, disability, ethnicity, family or marital status, gender identity or expression, language, national origin, physical and mental ability, political affiliation, religion, sexual orientation, socio-economic status, veteran status, and other characteristics that make them unique.

Community is at the heart of everything we do—from our writing and publishing programs to contributing to social enterprise nonprofits like reSET (www.resetco. org) and our work in founding B Local Connecticut.

We are endlessly grateful to our authors, readers, and local community for being the driving force behind the equitable and sustainable world we are building together.

To connect with us online or publish with us, visit us at www.publishyourpurpose.com.

Elevating Your Voice,

Jenn T Grace

Jenn T. Grace
Founder, Publish Your Purpose

www.ingramcontent.com/pod-product-compliance
Lightning Source LLC
Chambersburg PA
CBHW042313210326
41599CB00038B/7112